THE CONTENT ADVANTAGE

[Clout 2.0]

The Science of Succeeding
at Digital Business through
EFFECTIVE CONTENT

VOICES THAT MATTER™

COLLEEN JONES

The Content Advantage (Clout 2.0)
The Science of Succeeding at Digital Business through Effective Content, Second Edition

Colleen Jones

New Riders
www.newriders.com
Copyright © 2019 by Pearson Education, Inc. or its affiliates. All Rights Reserved.

New Riders is an imprint of Peachpit, an imprint of Pearson Education, Inc.
To report errors, please send a note to errata@peachpit.com

Executive Editor: Laura Norman
Development Editor: Robyn G. Thomas
Senior Production Editor: Tracey Croom
Copyeditor: Scout Festa
Compositor: Kim Scott, Bumpy Design
Proofer: Becky Winter
Indexer: Rebecca Plunkett
Cover Design: Mimi Heft
Interior Design: Kim Scott, Bumpy Design

ISBN-13: 978-0-13-515932-3
ISBN-10: 0-13-515932-6

1 18

To Chris for motivating me to think and do better

To Mom and Dad for their ardent support

In memory of my brother, Parker, the jester

ACKNOWLEDGMENTS

A book is by no means a solo endeavor. This second edition is anything but typical, so it required an outstanding team.

Nancy Davis spearheaded this second edition with enthusiasm. I thank the responsive team at New Riders, led by Laura Norman and Robyn Thomas, for being open to change and keeping this book on schedule.

I thank my amazing husband, Chris Jones, for his encouragement at the right moments and his patience with the extended hours that went into this edition. I also appreciate the overwhelming support from my parents, Jan and Pete, as well as my in-laws, Vivian and David.

I thank the content professionals that I've had the pleasure of meeting through training or consulting and through research about content for sharing their perspectives. You will hear from many of them in this edition.

CHAPTER REVIEWERS

I'm grateful that these talented thinkers and seasoned leaders took time out of their busy lives to give constructive feedback on chapters as they developed.[1]

- Andrea Sutton, Vice President of Design Technology at AT&T
- Jerele D. Neeld, Vice President of Globalization and Information Design at Dell EMC
- Scott Rosenberg, Senior Director of Global Marketing Operations and Governance at Visa
- Kate Kiefer Lee, Senior Director of Communications at MailChimp
- Jonathon Colman, Content Strategy Manager at Facebook
- Jennifer Hofer, Content Strategy Manager at Google
- Melinda Baker, Senior Marketing Director at American Cancer Society
- Susanna Guzman, Director of Web Services at CFA Institute
- Janice (Ginny) Redish, President at Redish & Associates and author of *Letting Go of the Words*
- Rachel Lovinger, Content Design Director at SapientRazorfish
- Jared Spool, Founder of User Interface Engineering and author of *Web Usability*
- Kristina Halvorson, CEO of Brain Traffic and author of *Content Strategy for the Web*
- Robert Mills, Content Strategist at GatherContent

---

1 The reviewers provided their individual opinions on their own time. Their participation does not necessarily reflect the opinions of their employers or an endorsement by their employers.

CONTENT SCIENCE TEAM

The core Content Science team contributed significantly to the research and insight reflected in this book. Andrew Johnson's analysis is second to none. I can't thank Lisa Clark enough for updating the visuals with her characteristic flair.

I appreciate Scott Abel and the Content Wrangler team as partners in recruiting research participants.

I also thank Content Science advisors and friends Toni Pashley, Senior Vice President at ShareCare, and David Forbes, Vice President at ASAP Solutions Group, for their insights and support.

ABOUT THE AUTHOR

Colleen Jones is the head of content at MailChimp, the marketing automation company recognized by Inc. as 2017 Company of the Year. A content expert and *Star Wars* fan, Colleen is also the founder of Content Science, a content strategy and intelligence firm where she advised or trained hundreds of the world's leading organizations to become Jedi Masters of digital content, including six of the Fortune 50, five of the largest United States web properties, three of the largest nonprofits, and three of the most trusted United States government agencies.

A passionate entrepreneur, Colleen led Content Science to develop the innovative content intelligence software ContentWRX, publish the online magazine *Content Science Review*, and offer online certifications through the Content Science Academy. These products are still empowering brands from American Cancer Society to AT&T to make content an influential force in accomplishing their goals.

Colleen has earned recognition as one of the Top 50 Most Influential Women in Content Marketing by a TopRank study, a Content Change Agent by *Society of Technical Communication's Intercom Magazine*, and one of the Top 50 Most Influential Content Strategists by multiple organizations. Colleen is a member of Mensa and an active supporter of women in technology. Colleen speaks at conferences and corporate events around the world, from San Francisco to Sydney.

CONTENTS

PERSUASION: OFFER EFFECTIVE AND INFLUENTIAL CONTENT

PRUDENCE: DEVELOP CONTENT INTELLIGENCE

POWER TO SCALE: MATURE CONTENT OPERATIONS

PRESCIENCE: THE CONTENT FUTURE

INTRODUCTION

● ●

This book is not so much a second edition as it is a start-to-finish revamp. My goal? To make *The Content Advantage* an updated go-to resource for you and your team. I'm sharing a few points of context that will help you get the most value from this book.

WHO THIS BOOK IS FOR

This book will benefit a variety of people who have a stake in content at a company, no matter whether that company is small, ginormous, or somewhere in between.

EXECUTIVES

You will gain understanding of the urgency to make content a core business competency. You also will gain insight into what it takes to define a content vision and strategy. And you will learn the value of content intelligence in making informed content decisions. To start (or to build on what you already started), this book also offers approaches and examples.

CONTENT MANAGERS AND PRACTITIONERS

This book offers arguments and talking points to justify starting or growing content efforts at your company. Additionally, you will get a variety of evidence-based approaches, examples, and tips that you can use or adapt to use at your company.

MANAGERS AND PRACTITIONERS IN RELATED DISCIPLINES

This book explains why content won't work well for you if it isn't a core competency at your company, with its own leadership and resources. You will gain empathy for the work involved in planning, creating, delivering, and optimizing effective content. You also will see the value in supporting your content co-workers as they advocate for maturing your company's content approach.

WHAT'S DIFFERENT ABOUT THIS SECOND EDITION

This edition is different in three main ways.

MORE CONTENT ANALYSIS AND CONTENT STRATEGY

In the first edition, I left the explanation of content analysis and content strategy up to other sources. But over the past eight years, I have experimented, along with the Content Science team, with approaches to content analysis and content strategy across many different organizations. I'm passing on many lessons learned in *The Content Advantage*.

Additionally, I include more analysis about why content is critical to digital business or, if you like, digital transformation. If you're making a case for content or for taking content to the next level, my hope is that this book will help.

CONTENT OPERATIONS DEMYSTIFIED

When I wrote the first edition, businesses other than magazines and newspapers hardly knew what an editorial calendar was. Now, we have companies such as Red Bull, which is a media company that sells some energy drinks, and Fitbit, which offers a system of wearable and home devices, applications, and personalized healthy-living content. While not every company has to go that far, every company will need the right content for the right customer in the right touchpoint at the right time. That takes not only content vision and strategy but also well-executed content operations. This edition covers issues that help companies align their content operations with their vision and strategy, such as content operations maturity, content intelligence, and content automation.

FRESH EXAMPLES AND A LOOK AHEAD

This edition updates examples of influential content from the first edition and introduces the dimensions of content effectiveness. Other examples appear throughout the book from industries ranging from credit monitoring to manufacturing to health and wellness to travel. This edition also offers a new perspective on the future of content.

WHAT THIS BOOK MEANS BY "SCIENCE"

I use "science" in the subtitle of this book and as a theme throughout. I also use it in the name of my company. Science has different meanings to different people, so let's clarify what I mean by science. I like the term because it connotes three distinct but complementary concepts—all of which work for content.

REFINING OR OPTIMIZING PRACTICE

When you say something like "she has that down to a science," you mean she has the practice optimized to some exactitude. She's an expert wielding her knowledge, process, and tools to perform at an expected level. She's also continually optimizing to improve performance.

In this spirit of science, this edition offers ways to get your company's content down to a science. I share methodologies, techniques, and examples supported by research.

OBSERVING AND DOCUMENTING

This aspect of science is watching and describing what you see. Observation alone teaches us what is happening in reality, even if we don't yet fully understand why. In fact, this effort often raises useful questions rather than providing complete answers. Primatologist and anthropologist Jane Goodall, marine biologist Rachel Carson, and science author Bill Bryson have all done extraordinary work in observing the world and communicating their thoughtful perspective.

With this sense of science in mind, I share throughout the book my perspective based on what I have observed in the wilds of doing content for

20 years in many contexts, as well as several anecdotes. Additionally, my observations have raised questions for me, which I have sought to answer with the third aspect of science.

EXPERIMENTING AND INNOVATING

This sense focuses on using what we know to develop ideas about why things happen and to develop predictions about what we don't know. This sense is the creative, problem-solving side of science. Geniuses Marie Curie and Stephen Hawking exemplify this type of science, with Marie Curie discovering radioactivity and Stephen Hawking advancing the theory of relativity and the field of quantum mechanics. This meaning of science involves developing a hypothesis, experimenting to discover whether the hypothesis is true, and learning enough over time to flesh out an existing theory—or to form a completely new one.

In this spirit of science, *The Content Advantage* offers insights into using content intelligence, or what you know, to make decisions about your content in the future. I borrow insight from poker and game theory and introduce the concept of becoming a content genius. Additionally, I point out the value of dedicating some of your content operations to innovation, and I share results from Content Science's own experiments.

This book draws on three senses of science and, consequently, is based on a range of evidence, including

- Research conducted by the Content Science team
- Research conducted by others
- My experience over two decades in a range of organizations
- The experience of other credible professionals and experts

HOW TO TAKE ADVANTAGE OF *THE CONTENT ADVANTAGE*

The first edition of this book lasted for eight years because readers held onto it as a useful reference. Few things made me happier than to sign a copy that was full of dog-eared pages and sticky notes. With this second edition, I aspired to make the book not only a long-lasting reference but also a useful, cohesive read or listen. To make the most of this book, I suggest that you

- First, read or listen to it from start to finish.
- Return to chapters or topics of immediate need or interest and use the references, checklists, or other resources offered.
- Keep the book on hand and revisit it regularly as you mature your content approach and different topics become important to you.

Content is science. In business, it's also a game. While no book can give you a cheat code to guarantee you win with every content effort, this book acts as a guide you can turn to again and again as you play. Over time, you will win more than you lose and, consequently, make your content an advantage.

PROBLEM: A NEW CROSSROADS

• •

We face a new content choice as digital business
becomes the rule, not the exception.

1 DIGITAL KEEPS DIVERTING THE ROAD TO SUCCESS

. . . .

The path to success is far from a straight line.

YOU STEP INTO THE ROAD, AND IF YOU DON'T KEEP YOUR FEET,
THERE IS NO KNOWING WHERE YOU MIGHT BE SWEPT OFF TO.

—J.R.R. Tolkien, *Lord of the Rings*

Let's start with a fact. I'd like you to guess the answer to this question:

What percentage of Fortune 500 companies have disappeared since the year 2000?

If you guessed a number around 50 percent or more, you are correct. If you did not, you're not alone. I was shocked to learn that such a high percentage of U.S. publicly traded companies had died or become absorbed by competitors. How could this happen? Many business experts and journalists agree that the most significant cause is digital disruption. Digital no longer means offering a website or a mobile application to complement offline operations. It means fundamentally changing the way companies do business, such as facing new competitors and responding to the wide-ranging impact of artificial intelligence, and other technological advances, just to survive, much less thrive.

The situation today reminds me of one of my favorite stories growing up, *Through the Looking-Glass and What Alice Found There*. At one point, Alice runs with the Red Queen for a long time and then realizes they are in the same spot as when they began.

> "Well, in our country," said Alice, still panting a little, "you'd generally get to somewhere else—if you run very fast for a long time, as we've been doing."
>
> "A slow sort of country!" said the Queen. "Now, here, you see, it takes all the running you can do, to keep in the same place. If you want to get somewhere else, you must run at least twice as fast as that!"

That seemed fascinatingly strange to me when I was a child. As an adult in the digital age, it rings true. Let's take a closer look at why and how digital is turning business into a Red Queen's race.

DIGITAL IS CHANGING BUSINESS FASTER AND MORE FREQUENTLY THAN EVER

One of the most useful resources I've found for understanding this current trend is the World Economic Forum, which is a Swiss nonprofit committed to improving the state of the world by engaging a wide variety of business and civic leaders at its annual forum and in ongoing reports. The theme of the 2016 forum was digital disruption (specifically the Fourth Industrial Revolution), where Accenture CEO Pierre Nanterme asserted the impact like this:

> Digital disruption is at the heart of all the conversations I have with CEOs today. And this is not surprising, as it presents the most significant threats and opportunities any of us have faced in business.
>
> When assessing the implications, consider the fact that new digital business models are the principal reason why just over half of the names of companies on the Fortune 500 have disappeared since the year 2000. And yet we are only at the beginning of what the World Economic Forum calls the "Fourth Industrial Revolution," characterized not only by mass adoption of digital technologies but by innovations in everything from energy to biosciences.[1]

As further evidence that digital disruption is causing our Fourth Industrial Revolution, consider these fascinating facts offered by *Fortune* from a survey of the 2017 Fortune 500 CEOs.

- 73 percent of CEOs surveyed identified the "rapid pace of technological change" as their biggest challenge.
- 71 percent of CEOs surveyed agreed with the statement "These days, I consider my company to be a technology company."
- 81 percent of CEOs surveyed considered artificial intelligence and machine learning as "very important" or "extremely important" to the future of the company—a huge increase from 54 percent in 2016.[2]

Just about every company, regardless of industry, has to be a digital company. Are companies putting their money where their digital concerns are? The answer seems to be yes. Analyst firm IDC reports that worldwide spend on digital transformation reached $1.1 trillion in 2017 alone and will hit $1.8 trillion in 2018, with $437 billion of that spend in the U.S.[3]

DIGITAL DISRUPTION IS HERE TO STAY

So digital disruption is not hype or a fluke. It's happening. It's also not likely to go away any time soon. In fact, it likely will intensify. The World Economic Forum has identified four waves, each marked by rapid change. Nanterme describes them like this:

We are seeing the Fourth Industrial Revolution emerge in a series of waves: the digital consumer, who enjoys more interactive and personalized experiences thanks to SMAC (social, mobile, analytics, and cloud) technologies; the digital enterprise, which leverages SMAC technologies to optimize the cost of corporate functions and to transform enterprise collaboration for greater productivity; and the emerging digital operations wave, where companies are truly revolutionizing business with the use of artificial intelligence, robotics, cognitive computing, and the Industrial Internet of Things.

And Nanterme goes on to explain the accelerated change:

The rapid pace and scale of disruption is unique to the Fourth Industrial Revolution. Digital companies can reach new customers immediately and at virtually zero marginal cost. They can compete in new sectors by collaborating with peers and competitors. They can massively improve quality and productivity by converging technologies and sources of data.

When I think of a company that is navigating digital disruption well, I think of Intuit. *Fortune* listed Intuit as number 537 on the 2017 Fortune 500 but as number 8 in the Future 50 Leaders list, a ranking of companies in terms of breakout growth potential. One reason for that 8 ranking is Intuit's capacity to change.[4] Intuit started as a disruptor itself with the release of Quicken, the desktop software for personal accounting, in 1993. Since then, Intuit has released a range of successful products while reinventing itself to navigate big challenges, such as

- Converting desktop software to web-based software and mobile applications
- Responding to threats from disruptors such as Mint.com, which tracks all your personal finance accounts in one place

So companies and organizations need to transform themselves digitally— likely multiple times, the way Intuit has—to survive, much less thrive, in the Fourth Industrial Revolution. What does that mean for getting results through digital? To start, it means avoiding mistakes.

THESE MISTAKES ARE STILL HAPPENING. AND STILL INSANE.

In the seven years since the first edition of this book, many companies continued to start and restart these paths to nowhere. These mistaken routes all miss the importance of content.

PUSHY TRICKS AND SMALL TWEAKS

Think about conversions, a critical result. To make a sale or get a lead, many websites use persuasion like a pushy salesperson, aiming high-pressure ploys at people as if they were stupid targets. One trick I love to hate is the countdown timer. Every tick of the timer tries to rush me into signing up.

Such tricks act like prods to push people along. Do they get results?

Many consultants say we should expect 2 to 3 percent of people who visit websites to convert (buy a product, for example). In fact, the global conversion rate, as noted by the Monetate Ecommerce Quarterly Index, still hovers around 2 to 4 percent. That rate range has not changed since 2003. Even if you consider that not everyone who visits an ecommerce website intends to buy, these rates are low. And they're not improving.

How can we improve? Many consultants tell us that testing and optimizing are the answer. We're encouraged to tweak the text, buttons, and pictures on our websites and landing pages until conversion rates rise. (That's sometimes where manipulative tricks come in too.) We've had years to experiment. If tricks and tweaks worked so well, the global conversion rate would have improved, if not skyrocketed, by now.

Should you stop testing or stop optimizing? No. But that shouldn't be all you do. Tricks and tweaks, by themselves, are not enough to get meaningful results.

OVERPROMISED TECHNOLOGY

No IT product, feature, or widget alone will give you results. I don't care what the smiley vendor with the slick demo and the free drinks says. Tom Davenport, an industry analyst and author, has pointed out the limits of technology:

The important point, however, is that we need more naysayers in the IT field… Most products don't work as advertised or very well in general, and even more are unworthy of the hype that surrounds them.

Time and again, I've watched companies, especially big ones, look to a product, platform, or technology trend such as artificial intelligence or digital core transformation as the pill to cure all ills. Time and again, I've watched those companies try to launch that panacea through a doomed project. Recent studies by the cloud technology company Innotas show that more than half of such technology projects fail. Those projects remind me a lot of this *Dilbert* cartoon (**Figure 1.1**), where a technology initiative starts with promising everything and ends by delivering nothing.

Figure 1.1: Many IT projects start with unrealistic expectations and end in disappointment.

SEO SNAKE OIL

A cousin of overpromised technology, SEO snake oil is the promise of high search engine rankings with little effort. Who sells it? Slippery SEO consultants who take advantage of the fact that search engine formulas aren't public. They're held more sacred than your grandmother's secret recipe. Those formulas also change regularly. So no one, including consultants, knows exactly what ranks your website. The snake oil consultants "guarantee" rankings and make dubious recommendations. One of my favorites is to post lots of articles crammed with keywords. The result is often gibberish. And these consultants insist the effort is worth spending a chunk of change.

But there is legitimate SEO work being done by good SEO consultants. They experiment with different variables and observe what affects your search engine rankings. They pay attention when Google releases changes to its algorithm, and they warn that spammy, outdated SEO practices will be punished with lower rankings. Mostly, good design and content go a long way toward good SEO.

I don't mean you should throw out SEO concerns. However, SEO snake oil leads people to spend money on being found (which often doesn't work) at the expense of making their content and overall digital presence worth finding. If your website is mired in meaningless articles "for SEO purposes," you're not going to get results.

GRAPHIC AND INTERACTION DESIGN ALONE

An eye-catching and easy-to-use digital experience is good. But is that all you need for results?

Graphic Design Helps But Isn't Enough

Good graphic design gives people a fantastic first impression so that they don't leave your website right away. It also helps set your style. Those benefits are valuable but, by themselves, don't sustain results for the long term. How many beautiful websites have you visited once and then forgotten? Oh wait, you probably don't remember.

Usability and Interaction Are Important, But You Need More

Deeper design, such as whether a website or other digital touchpoint has a user-friendly interface, is important. If people can't interact well with you online, you have a major problem. Usability is even a common courtesy that will help your reputation. But this deeper design does not fully address the substance of most content.

SHORTSIGHTED MARKETING

These problems happen in the name of marketing.

Broadcasting Doesn't Work for the Interactive Digital Space

Since the late 1990s, marketing has claimed to adapt to the web. Before then, marketing followed a broadcast model, which treated the company brand as a battleship blasting its message at targets (the customers). Usually, the blasts were campaigns or promotions that lasted for a few weeks or months.

Although marketers still talk about companies becoming interactive, it largely hasn't happened. A 2010 *Harvard Business Review* article called for the complete reinvention of marketing and states.

> To compete in this aggressively interactive environment, companies must shift their focus from driving transactions to maximizing customer lifetime value. That means making products and brands subservient to long-term customer relationships.

Most marketers I encounter still blast a message at customers rather than plan to interact with customers for the long term.

Online Ads Are Often Ineffectual

Banner ads. Pop-up windows. Distracting videos. Overpromising click-baity search engine ads. Online ads are so bad, they're infamous. It's easy to blame the designers or marketers. But the real problem is with the online advertising system that has promised from the beginning to provide better data about advertising effectiveness than do other advertising methods. Since the first edition of this book, an incredible amount of data about online advertising has become available. And that data is telling us that online advertising has little effect or that we are still uncertain about the effect.

For example, last year eBay released an extensive study in partnership with a group of respected economists about the effectiveness of search engine advertising. The sobering conclusion? That search engine advertising is useless and unprofitable for a prominent, well-known brand.[5]

As another example, the largest U.S. advertiser, Procter & Gamble, cut $140 million in digital ad spending last year because of concerns that bots drove fake traffic to the ads and that ads displayed on websites and applications undermined their product brands.[6] Seeing an advertisement for an Olay lotion on a porn website or a controversial political website, for example, would be a problem. To boot, Procter & Gamble's chief brand officer, Marc Pritchard, led an intense campaign demanding significantly improved transparency and adherence to standards from digital agencies and from advertising platforms such as Google and Facebook. Although Pritchard sees promise for "the next generation" of digital advertising, it's clear that online advertising often overpromises and underdelivers.

I could go on, and I bet you could add to this list of tried-and-still-untrue solutions. Now, new tempting but mistaken paths have emerged.

THESE NEW MISTAKES ARE LEADING ORGANIZATIONS DOWN THE WRONG PATH

Two mistakes, design thinking and content bloat, either overlook content in a new way or focus on the wrong aspects of content.

THINKING THAT DESIGN THINKING WILL SAVE YOU

When I wrote the first edition of this book, "design thinking" was emerging as a buzzword in the business world to refer to applying a mix of research and design principles to identifying and solving business problems. Design thinking is still a hot concept, especially at large companies, resulting in extensive training for a wide range of non-designers in design. But as with technology, design thinking is not a panacea, because it leaves out other important thinking.

What thinking is left out? User experience design pioneer and Adaptive Path founder Peter Merholz tells us in his concise yet prescient article for *Harvard Business Review* "Why Design Thinking Won't Save You."[7] Merholz notes that Adaptive Path succeeded because of the diverse thinking assembled. Design thinking does not account for, among other things

- Business thinking, which is still critical
- Anthropology and sociology research thinking
- Library science/information architecture thinking

That last item is where Merholz touches on content, and today I would add a host of content-related considerations outlined in the rest of this book. I also would add marketing and technology thinking. Merholz humorously takes the need for so much different thinking to its logical conclusion:

> All of these disciplinary backgrounds allow people to bring distinct perspectives to our work, allowing for insights that wouldn't be achieved if we were all cut from the same cloth. Do we need to espouse "library thinking," "history thinking," and "arts thinking?" Should we look at Steve Jobs's background, and say what business needs is more "calligraphic thinking"?

> Obviously, this is getting absurd, but that's the point. The supposed dichotomy between "business thinking" and "design thinking" is foolish. It's like the line from The Blues Brothers, in response to the question "What kind of music do you usually have here?" The woman responds, "We got both kinds. We got country and western." Instead, what we must understand is that in this savagely complex world, we need to bring as broad a diversity of viewpoints and perspectives to bear on whatever challenges we have in front of us. While it's wise to question the supremacy of "business thinking," shifting the focus only to "design thinking" will mean you're missing out on countless possibilities.

I suspect that advocates of the design thinking hype cannot or will not share Merholz's foresight, and so his article perhaps did not garner as much attention as it deserves. His contrarian view is worth revisiting. Over the past several years, I have seen first-hand the consequences of the misguided supremacy of design thinking, including

- Poor treatment of content professionals by designers, such as not including them in processes or respecting their feedback
- Disagreements and delays in decisions due to lack of collaboration between the designers and the business leaders
- Designs developed with a complete lack of awareness of the implications for content, such as assuming that a repository of content existed that did not
- Leaving content strategy or content marketing strategy professionals out of efforts to define product or experience strategy
- Design executives and professionals viewing content as a discipline that design has to subsume, not as a critical business capacity that needs its own leadership and operations

And I'm only scratching the surface. The point here is that design thinking alone will not suffice to navigate the road to business success that digital constantly disrupts.

CREATING CONTENT BLOAT BY FOCUSING ON CONTENT QUANTITY

I am delighted to say that since the first edition of this book more organizations and individuals have turned their attention to content. It is no coincidence that the internet is now doubling in size every two years, resulting in 50-fold growth of content and data from 2011 to 2020. I am not saying this book alone spurred this newfound attention to content. My point is that more organizations are now aware of content and doing something about it. Many have achieved important successes, as you'll see later in this book. At the same time, many companies have fallen for the "more is better" philosophy on content, creating a high volume of content across a variety of digital touchpoints.

For instance, in 2015 the technology giant Intel found itself suffering from what I call content bloat, with content feeding 12,500 pages on the main website, 715 microsites, 324 social handles, and 38 mobile applications.[8] And you can imagine the number of images, PDFs, videos, and other digital assets composing that content. This volume causes a number of problems for customers or users and the companies creating and managing the content, as you can see in **Table 1.1**.

Table 1.1 Sample Problems with the Content Volume Play

FOR CUSTOMERS / USERS	FOR COMPANIES OFFERING THE CONTENT
Findability	**Complexity**
Quality, relevant content becomes increasingly hard to find or discover.	Content assets and digital touchpoints become increasingly challenging and expensive to manage and scale.
Confusion + Mistrust	**Inefficiency**
Content gives conflicting messages, is outdated, makes completing tasks difficult, or uses an inconsistent voice.	Sections of redundant content are created by different groups and compete with each other for visibility in search listings.
Dissatisfaction	**Ineffectiveness**
Content does not help and even hinders new and existing customers, leading to low satisfaction with the customer experience.	Content is not attracting the right people, encouraging self-service, improving conversions, or otherwise supporting business objectives.

If you care about content but have found that your organization has followed a path similar to Intel, the good news is that you can course correct.
As Intel's director of digital governance, Scott Rosenberg led a multiyear
effort to reduce content based on clear standards and guidelines for effectiveness, and then introduced governance to prevent content bloat from
happening again. Rosenberg notes

> The first step in your digital governance journey should be to deeply
> understand what it is you're trying to address and the business impact.
> For example, if you are tackling content strategy issues like content
> bloat or what I call "experience bloat" (an abundance of websites, social
> handles, mobile apps, etc.), clearly define the impact to your marketing
> objectives and customer experience. Is it diluting your brand value?
> Decreasing qualified leads? Exposing internal organizational silos to
> your customers? Once done, share and validate your findings within
> your organization's key influential stakeholders, such as your CMO and
> executive team. Gaining senior buy-in across the company is critical to
> securing the support, resources, and widespread behavioral shift needed
> to build a strong digital governance framework.

The rest of this book will help you avoid content bloat or course correct it.

SUMMARY

Thanks to digital disruption, we all face a new, often changing, path to
success. Attempting the same shortcuts will disappoint, and we face new
tempting but mistaken paths that are really dead ends. To survive, much
less thrive, in the digital age, businesses need to rethink their approach
to content.

REFERENCES

1 "Digital disruption has only just begun" www.weforum.org/agenda/2016/01/
   digital-disruption-has-only-just-begun/

2 "Fortune 500 CEOs See A.I. as a Big Challenge" http://fortune.com/2017/06/08/
   fortune-500-ceos-survey-ai/

3 "IDC Forecasts Worldwide Spending on Digital Transformation Technologies to
   Reach $1.3 Trillion in 2018" www.idc.com/getdoc.jsp?containerId=prUS43381817

4 "The Future 50 List" http://fortune.com/future-50/

5 "Consumer Heterogeneity and Paid Search Effectiveness: A Large Scale Field
   Experiment" www.nber.org/papers/w20171.pdf

6   "Procter & Gamble Cut Up to $140 Million in Ad Spending Because of Brand Safety Concerns" www.adweek.com/digital/procter-gamble-cut-140-million-in-digital-ad-spending-because-of-brand-safety-concerns/

7   "Why Design Thinking Won't Save You," Peter Merholz. *Harvard Business Review.* https://hbr.org/2009/10/why-design-thinking-wont-save

8   "Intel Addresses Modern Marketing Challenges through Digital Governance" https://review.content-science.com/2016/10/intel-addresses-modern-marketing-challenges-through-digital-governance/

2　DO CONTENT WELL OR DIE

• •

The shift of business to digital has made content critical.

THE BIGGEST RISK IS NOT TAKING ANY RISK. IN A WORLD
THAT'S CHANGING REALLY QUICKLY, THE ONLY STRATEGY THAT
IS GUARANTEED TO FAIL IS NOT TAKING RISKS.

—Mark Zuckerberg

HOPE.

—Princess Leia Organa

With the rise of digital, I'm convinced we have entered a new business era: the content era. We're living in a time in which content is both essential for business survival and a potential business advantage. Let's take a closer look at why.

DIGITAL BUSINESS CUSTOMERS ARE SUBSCRIBERS

Business has evolved from a pay-per-product model to a subscription model, or what many call the *subscription economy*. Credit Suisse, a financial services company, found that people spent $40.2 billion on subscriptions in 2015 alone, which is almost double what people spent on subscriptions in 2000. Jason Pressman of Shasta Ventures puts it like this:

> These days, it's almost more unusual not to do a subscription business than to do one. Startups and legacy businesses alike are experimenting with what's possible in vertical industries that didn't seem feasible before. Take Cadillac, which recently launched a program allowing drivers to drive multiple models for $1500 a month.[1]

Subscriptions give customers flexibility and affordability while they give businesses dependable revenue. And the continued digital disruption drives even more creative experimentation with subscriptions. For example, the Internet of Things trend is connecting devices or equipment to the Internet. Even a refrigerator. That means that any device or equipment can turn into a subscription. Have you heard of the spinning bike called Peloton? If not, chances are you will soon. It's a spinning bike equipped with detailed performance analytics, and it requires a yearly subscription to online, interactive spinning classes for a wide range of levels. Customers buy the bike once and renew the subscription on a regular basis. Already successful, Peloton secured extensive funding in 2017 from investors who anticipate that Peloton will become a billion-dollar business. Noted investor Mary Meekins says that "Peloton is supporting especially broad subscriber engagement and growth. We believe Peloton is the leader in a new business that has significant potential: physical interactive media."

Physical interactive media means a device (the bike) and a subscription to… drum roll… content.

CUSTOMERS NEED CONTENT

Regardless whether you consider your customers to be subscribers, they need content throughout their relationship with your company. The need for content in a variety of touchpoints, from websites to personal assistants to print to even bikes, never stops (**Figure 2.1**). You must attract customers, convert them into buyers, and retain them.

Figure 2.1: Businesses need content to win over and keep subscribers.

ATTRACT CUSTOMERS

Businesses can attract customers by educating or entertaining them with content. For example, American Express Open Forum offers a wealth of articles and videos with practical advice and inspirational stories to help small businesses grow stronger. This content positions American Express as a trusted advisor early in the customer relationship.

CONVERT CUSTOMERS

A wide range of research shows that people research most purchases—whether for personal or business situations—online (see numerous reports at ecommercefoundation.org). So businesses must provide content about their products and services to address questions, explain the features or specifications, and reiterate the benefit or value in clear and compelling ways.

RETAIN CUSTOMERS

Content can play many important roles, from adding educational value to being the main product or service offering to enabling customer success.

American Express Open Forum continues to offer value to small business owners after they become customers. That means American Express gets additional return from investing in that content.

Content is a centerpiece for Peloton in the form of online spinning classes with instructor personalities and customer performance analytics. Similarly, any media company, from social to traditional, depends on content as its main offering.

Blasting the Myth That People Don't Read

"Just post it—no one will read it anyway."

If anyone has said that to you as an excuse not to spend time on web content, especially text, then take heart. Research is on your side. The Poynter EyeTrack study shows that people actually read more deeply online than offline.

Where did this myth come from? One source is misinterpretation of Jakob Nielsen's study "Concise, SCANNABLE, and Objective: How to Write for the Web." Nielsen asserts that people mostly scan when they are online.

So who is right? In short, everyone is right. People scan until they find the content that is relevant to them. Once they find it, they will read deeply. If they don't find relevant content, they won't ever read deeply. So offering relevant content is a huge opportunity to influence people.

And content such as dynamic contextual help, clear instructions and guides, and troubleshooting repositories help customers help themselves 24/7. For example, the fitness equipment manufacturing company Precor revamped their welcome kit for customers to ensure successful setup.[2] As another example, Intuit carefully incorporated clear yet friendly instructions and dynamic help in the revamp of TurboTax, to much acclaim.[3]

So customers need content in every phase of their relationship with a business. Piece of cake, right? Not exactly.

CONTENT IS STILL HARD

Although more organizations are making an effort at content than ever before, I would be lying if I said content has become easier. A content approach that meets customers' high expectations still does not come from fairy dust, no matter how hard you wish for it.

GREAT (AND EVOLVING) EXPECTATIONS

Companies such as Netflix and Amazon increasingly raise the bar for customer experience. As a result, millions of people have become accustomed to relevant and even personalized content being easy to find and consume.

Further, companies such as Netflix, Hulu, and Peloton now offer original programming informed by data, setting new standards for engaging, entertaining, and quality content. Netflix pioneered this direction by taking a chance on the immensely successful *House of Cards*.

As if that weren't enough, products such as FitBit, Under Armour's My Fitness Pal, and TurboTax are innovating the quality and relevance of educational and customer success content. I already mentioned TurboTax's approach, so let's talk more about My Fitness Pal and FitBit. Those experiences bring together user data, content, and artificial intelligence to create highly dynamic personalized experiences. (We'll take a closer look at how such companies innovate in the next few chapters.) Heck, even the Dollar Shave Club offers a handy little magazine with each delivery.

If you think this kind of innovation is limited to big brands, think again. My favorite spinning class studio, called Burn, models the potential for content in a digital business. I go to the Burn website to buy a package of classes or subscribe. Also using the website, I register for a class and select the exact seat I want. When I arrive at the studio, I check in using a kiosk. During the class, my bike collects all of my performance data, such as revolutions per minute, estimated calories burned, power output, and more. If I give permission, I can have that data display on a digital sign at the front of the classroom to see how I compare to the rest of the class. (I'm usually in the middle at the start of a class, and seeing that gives me some extra motivation to try to move up a notch or two.) Cool, right? But what really caught my attention was this. After my first class, I received an amazing email within two minutes. The email congratulated me and summarized my performance, including rank, calories, power output, and more. I literally said, "Wow!" (**Figure 2.2**). This single-location spinning studio delivers a stellar content-rich digital experience that many large companies cannot. In fact, small businesses can use content as a big advantage in the digital business age, as we'll explore further in the rest of this book.

My point here is that your customers likely encounter many such standard-setting companies, big and small. That means your customers' expectations for content are high and becoming higher. So it's no wonder many organizations struggle to meet those expectations.

CHALLENGES TO MEET EXPECTATIONS

Why is content so challenging? To help answer that question, my firm Content Science conducted studies in 2015 and 2017 with nearly 200 content professionals in a variety of industries.[4,5] Our surveys and interviews revealed these top challenges (**Figure 2.3**).

These challenges fall into three basic categories:

1. Lack of content vision and strategy
2. Limited access to data and experimentation
3. Outdated content operations (including technology)

Figure 2.2: A small spinning studio delivers a big wow moment.

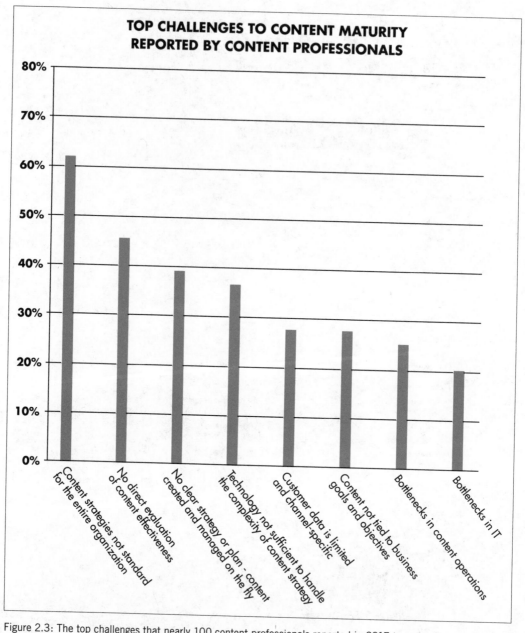

Figure 2.3: The top challenges that nearly 100 content professionals reported in 2017 to maintain or improve their organization's content approach

Lack of Content Vision and Strategy

Many organizations still have not defined a vision for their content—or for the future state. In our 2017 study, 55 percent of respondents said their organization had no content vision. Consequently, it's impossible to define a strategy (or combination of strategies) for achieving the vision and involve all the right people. I like how Tina Keister of Teladoc, who participated in the study, articulates this point:

> If you don't know what success looks like, you can't make it happen. If you all have a different idea in your head of what success is, you'll actually be sabotaging each other simply because you don't have a shared vision.

In my experience, the main cause for little content vision and strategy is no leadership. I have watched well-intentioned companies flounder for years with content because they would not commit to hiring a content leader or executive.

Limited Access to Data and Experimentation

This challenge happens in organizations of all sizes. I once worked with a large conglomerate possessing perhaps the world's largest data lake, yet the content teams had little to no data about their content's effectiveness. Talk about irony!

Our 2017 study found that content professionals who reported the ability to evaluate content's impact and the freedom to experiment with content options were significantly more likely to report content success. Why is that? One study participant put it like this:

> It's hard not to salivate over some organizations and what they've done, these new innovations. It's clear just from what they're doing that these organizations truly invest in their content. They're fully committed to and understand the value of content, and you can see it just in the number of things they're trying, even if some of them fail. I think if that level of understanding or investment is there, companies are able to go a lot further.

When you have the freedom to evaluate different approaches to content, you will be more likely to figure out what approach works and why.

Outdated Content Operations

It's not hard to understand why this challenge occurs. Without a vision for the content future and data to understand the impact of content in the present, there isn't much reason to change content operations. Why fix what no one thinks is broken?

Our study found that content professionals who are evolving content roles, embracing content automation, and exploring the best ways to use artificial intelligence were significantly more likely to report success. Study participant Noel McDonagh of Dell EMC explains:

> AI and machine learning are the only way we're going to be able to deal with the fact that the demand for content is increasing exponentially. We're going to have to automate the production of certain aspects of content.

Even though doing content well is hard, it is achievable. To help, this book devotes space to developing a content vision, a strategy (or set of strategies) to achieve it, and the application of techniques and operations to execute it effectively. My intention in this book will help you make progress and aid you in educating your leadership or stakeholders.

By now, I hope it's clear that you cannot do digital business without doing content well. Your organization faces a choice. Invest in content strategy and operations as you undergo digital transformation. Or disappear.

If you choose the latter, then you can stop here. The former? The rest of this book will help you take a more strategic and systematic approach to content. The framework and principles I share are based on working with organizations ranging from niche retailers to huge conglomerates. No matter what size your organization is, you will gain value from this book.

REFERENCES

1 "The Not-So-New Promise of the Subscription Economy" www.forbes.com/sites/valleyvoices/2017/05/17/not-so-new-promise-of-subscription-economy/#564d13b44343

2 "How Precor Transformed an Editorial Process into a Business Asset" https://review.content-science.com/2017/11/how-precor-transformed-an-editorial-process-into-a-business-asset/

3 "How TurboTax Used Design to Win the Tax Wars" www.fastcodesign.com/3056784/how-turbotax-used-design-to-win-the-tax-wars

4 "What Makes Content Teams Thrive?" *Content Science Review*, https://content-science.com/professional-services/capabilities/content-teams-study/

5 "Content Operations + Leadership Benchmark Study" *Content Science Review*, https://content-science.com/professional-services/capabilities/content-operations-study/

PLAN: CONSTRUCT CONTENT STRATEGY AND TACTICS

· ·

Take control of content's role in your digital business.

3 DEVELOP A CONTENT VISION

· ·

Define a vision to inspire and guide yourself as well as your stakeholders, partners, and team.

"WOULD YOU TELL ME, PLEASE, WHICH WAY I OUGHT TO GO FROM HERE?"
"THAT DEPENDS A GOOD DEAL ON WHERE YOU WANT TO GET TO," SAID THE CAT.
"I DON'T MUCH CARE WHERE—" SAID ALICE.
"THEN IT DOESN'T MATTER WHICH WAY YOU GO," SAID THE CAT.

—Lewis Carroll, *Alice's Adventures in Wonderland*

Doing content well starts not with strategy but with vision. Let's explore content vision and how you can develop one.

CONTENT VISION IS YOUR FUTURE DESTINATION

Ever since Stephen Covey's *The Seven Habits of Highly Effective People* rocked the business world, vision has been important to business. Covey notes

> All things are created twice—first mentally, then physically. The key to creativity is to begin with the end in mind, with a vision and a blueprint of the desired result.

In today's digital business world, I would change "physically" to "physically or digitally." Content is so important to business now that it merits a vision. Content vision is the future state you aspire to. Without a clear idea of where you want to go, you cannot form a strategy to get there.

I confess I somewhat stumbled onto the need for content vision about a year after releasing the first edition of this book. I was working with a 200-year-old book publisher on content strategy for their website. To kick off the effort, I interviewed the publisher's leaders in marketing, product management, and user experience. I asked each leader, "What is your vision for the content?"

Most leaders did not have an answer, saying something like "I haven't really thought about it before." And those who did answer had very different, conflicting ideas for the vision. For example, one leader had exciting aspirations for the website to act less like an online book store and more like a gateway to useful and interesting knowledge in a variety of formats, not just books. Another leader desired improved and more consistent copywriting.

"Uh oh," I thought. "This stuff just got real. Real complicated."

After spending a few days figuring out how to come up with content strategy to support a cloudy vision, I had chewed my pen cap until it was only a few shreds of plastic. Fortunately, the publisher agreed to take a step back and work on defining a content vision before we attempted to form a content strategy. Ever since, I have experimented with and studied content vision. In our most recent study, we found 73 percent of content teams who reported success had defined and gained buy-in to a content vision. My hope is to save you and your pen caps from the same stress.

SIX ELEMENTS OF CONTENT VISION

Through a combination of my experience and talking to a variety of content professionals, I have identified some key elements that tend to make a content vision work well:

- **V**ivid
- **I**nspirational
- **S**ignificant
- **I**nfectious
- **O**ut of the Ordinary
- **N**orth Star

VIVID

I find that content planning can be either extremely conceptual and abstract or extremely tactical. Either extreme is difficult to picture. So your content vision will benefit from being descriptive, something that your team, your executives, and your stakeholders can easily understand and even visualize.

One way to start that description is to think about your content as a trusted advisor (**Figure 3.1**). For example, if you work in the food and beverage industry, a potential starting point for your content vision might be an enthusiastic chef or a health-conscious nutritionist.

Your content vision doesn't have to be anthropomorphized, though. I've partnered with clients to define vision summaries such as

- "The outfitter for foot health and comfort"
- "Thriving hub connecting people and knowledge"
- "World-class investment media integrated into our members' daily workflow"
- "The *Harvard Business Review* of content"
- "The Sanjay Gupta of foot health"

Those descriptions worked too. Your description will be different, of course, but what matters is making it vivid enough for people to start picturing it.

Figure 3.1: Examples of trusted advisors who can inspire content vision

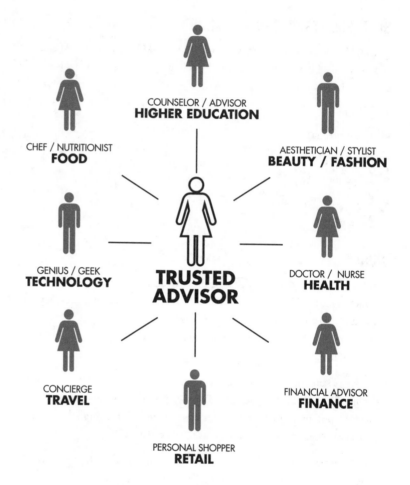

INSPIRATIONAL AND SIGNIFICANT

Your vision isn't to prevent typos. Your vision isn't to produce more video. Your content vision is something meaningful to your organization and your team and something ambitious enough that people will be motivated to put in extra effort to achieve it.

For example, maintaining a company blog just wasn't motivating enough for us, especially me, at Content Science to do an excellent job. However, aspiring to be the *Harvard Business Review* of content to change the world was. Within a few months of converting our blog into an online magazine called *Content Science Review*, we exceeded our initial goals for traffic and won a few awards. And today we're publishing our own insights about broad and deep topics and research, as well as exciting contributions from leading companies around the globe, such as Alibaba, Dun and Bradstreet, WebMD, the Coca-Cola Company, Airbnb, and more. A year ago, if you had told me we would achieve so much so quickly, I would have chuckled. My point here is that you can achieve more than you think possible with an inspirational and significant content vision.

INFECTIOUS AND OUT OF THE ORDINARY

Strive to make your content vision a unique idea that catches on easily. Ideally, your content vision will be a concept that people within your organization—and maybe even outside it—can "get" quickly and discuss enthusiastically. For instance, when Marriott announced its new content studio, the hotel brand also revealed that it seeks to be "the Red Bull of travel and hospitality." What does that mean? Red Bull embraced content early and built a wealth of unique media around adrenaline-inducing sports, events, and activities, such as extreme mountain biking. In the process, Red Bull has grown a loyal audience and come to consider itself not only a beverage manufacturer but also a media house. Marriott meant that they have similarly serious content ambitions. Marriott's vision was bold, unique for the hotel industry, and caught on quickly, even earning a mention in *Variety*.[1]

NORTH STAR

Finally, think of your content vision as a North Star. Try defining the vision as a guiding light through the craziness of the change and effort that are necessary to achieve your vision. When stakeholders or team members start to doubt or to suggest activities that don't fit your content strategy or roadmap, you have your vision to lead everyone back to the right focus.

As an example, Carrie Hane led a web transformation, including content transformation, at the American Society for Civil Engineers. I talked with her about the secrets to her success, and she coined a term that cracks me up: strategically nagging. What did Hane mean by that? The importance of reminding everyone involved of their goals and focus. So your content vision is a North Star that will help you strategically nag until your vision becomes reality.

In addition to considering these six elements, you can take steps to solidify and gain buy-in to the content vision.

HOW TO CRYSTALLIZE A CONTENT VISION

Chances are that content at your organization involves more than one person, as it did at the esteemed publisher I mentioned earlier. You can take steps to involve more people and crystallize the vision.

CONDUCT A CONTENT VISION WORKSHOP

Organize a workshop early in the planning process. The purpose of the workshop is to explore and start to define the vision. You might not reach a final vision, and that's OK. But what you *will* do is reconcile major discrepancies. People who are "thinking small" and have a limited view of content's potential will start to see more exciting possibilities. People who are "thinking big" about the content's future will start to recognize the change needed to make that future a reality. This alignment helps motivate everyone to support the content effort from the beginning.

Who to Invite

Invite content leaders. Content leaders might be the official managers or executives. They also might be people who do not have an official leadership title but are content leaders in terms of their thinking and influence.

Also consider inviting leaders who will ultimately need to support the content effort. Depending on your organization, these leaders might be in marketing, design, product, customer experience, and even technology.

What to Do

I like to spend one to two hours on activities that reveal people's perceptions of the current state and their aspirations for the future. Here are a few questions to drive activities and subsequent discussion, and you will probably think of others:

- What are three words that describe the content as it is today? Why?
- What are three words that describe the content as you want it to be in one to two years? Why?
- What are three great content examples? Why are they great?
- What is the maturity level of our content operations? Why?

If you're focused on content for a particular situation, such as a specific person or channel or product, then you can scope these activities accordingly.

After working through the questions, I like to spend an hour reviewing the elements of an effective content vision and then collaborating to define a *content vision statement*:

In x [time], our content will be y.

For example, in one year our blog will be the *Harvard Business Review* of content, offering inspiration, research, and practical advice to highly engaged content professionals.

This statement does not have to be final, but it should be a significant step toward clarifying the content direction. If participants get stuck, you can offer them some techniques to use. One of my favorites is to take a leading content example from a completely different industry and apply it to yours. Marriott did this with aspiring to be the Red Bull of travel.

You can adapt these activities for large groups by having attendees divide into groups of three or four, do the activity, and then come back together and discuss as one large group.

REFINE AND ILLUSTRATE THE VISION

After the workshop, you can refine the vision statement, if needed, so it has more of the six elements I described earlier. Also consider whether communicating about the vision would benefit from a visual, such as the simple example shown in **Figure 3.2**. You can use visuals of inspirational examples discussed in the workshop. Or you also can draft an early concept that illustrates the direction. If you develop a concept, be sure to clarify that it is only a concept and not a final approach, or else well-intentioned stakeholders could become distracted by the wording and details shown in the concept.

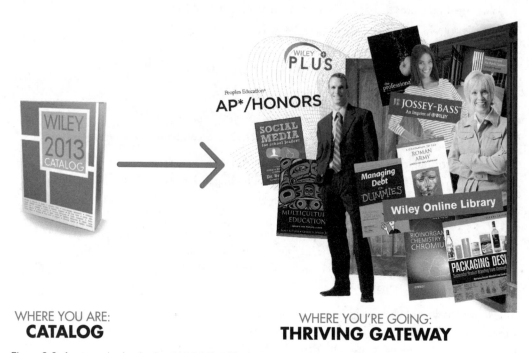

WHERE YOU ARE:
CATALOG

WHERE YOU'RE GOING:
THRIVING GATEWAY

Figure 3.2: An example simple visual (right) that illustrates a new vision for the existing content (left)

TAKE THE VISION ON A ROAD SHOW

If you work in a large organization, consider taking the vision on a road show. Meet with your boss, your team, and key stakeholders, most of whom should have participated in the workshop to discuss the updated content vision. This effort will prove to everyone that their feedback was heard and that it mattered. Few things motivate people more than seeing that their efforts had an impact on progress.

Additionally, the discussions will likely result in refinement of the vision and raise questions that will be useful to address in the rest of your planning. For example, one large company I worked with developed a content vision that depended heavily on personalization, which led to important questions about what customer data was available to drive it. Raising those questions early allowed the company to factor the questions into their content analysis, which we discuss in the next chapter. Your vision and the questions raised might be different, but the benefits you enjoy by raising questions early will be the same.

Effective content starts not with strategy but with a vision that is clear, ambitious, and unique. If you take the time to define a content vision, don't be surprised if next year at this time you look back and think, "Wow. We achieved even more than we first thought possible." Now, let's turn from thinking about the future state to understanding the current state through analysis.

REFERENCES

1 "How Marriott Wants to Be the Red Bull of the Hotel Industry" http://variety.com/2014/biz/news/how-marriott-wants-to-be-the-red-bull-of-the-hotel-industry-1201316184/

4 ANALYZE YOUR CONTENT, CUSTOMERS, AND CONTEXT

• •

Understand your current situation so you can plan the right change.

CHANGE BRINGS OPPORTUNITIES. ON THE OTHER HAND,
CHANGE CAN BE CONFUSING.
  —Michael Porter

YOU CAN'T STOP THE CHANGE, ANY MORE THAN YOU
CAN STOP THE SUNS FROM SETTING.
  —Shmi Skywalker

In Chapter 3, we walked through envisioning your content future. Now, let's consider why and how to assess your content present.

WHY ANALYZE THE CURRENT STATE

Never advise or decide on a content strategy without assessing the current state. Sometimes, companies question whether the assessment is necessary, especially if they are eager to make a big change or do not have much existing content. You might question the need for such analysis or, if you're already convinced, face the question yourself. So I'm sharing a few reasons why your organization needs to conduct this analysis.

PREVENT YOUR CONTENT STRATEGY FROM FAILING

If I had to pick the top reason businesses fail at content, I'd say it's because they don't have an accurate understanding of their content situation to inform their strategy. Such organizations build their strategy on a house of cards that, sooner or later, collapses. For example, I once worked with an online retailer that reached out after they tried to do thought leadership content, or content to advise and guide potential and existing customers, but did not get results. The company assumed that because they knew how to develop great sales content, they could also develop great thought leadership content. In our analysis, we discovered that customers felt the thought leadership content was too pushy and focused on sales. The retailer could have avoided this misstep—which involved revamping hundreds of content assets—by analyzing the situation first.

Businesses often suffer from delusions of content grandeur or delusions of content failure—or perhaps both, if content stakeholders have different and conflicting perspectives. These delusions can lead to a content strategy that fails.

Delusions of Content Grandeur

Companies, or teams within a company, sometimes see the existing content through rose-colored glasses, thinking it's much more important or impactful than it is. For example, you would be amazed at how attached companies can become to mediocre corporate blogs. Inertia also comes into play here; people prefer to maintain the status quo rather than make a change, so they cling to any reason to do so.

A related delusion I encounter is about content capacity. Company executives repeatedly overestimate their ability to sustain a sophisticated content strategy over time without making changes to content operations, such as hiring the right people or improving processes. (Last I checked, content is still not created and delivered by the content fairy!) And content teams are feeling the pain of this delusion. In Content Science's 2017 study of content operations, 53 percent of participants (content team leaders and members) reported that they did not know the budget for content. How can a company plan realistically for a new approach to content without knowing the existing budget and planning how it will change?[1]

Although an extreme delusion of content grandeur can lead to misguided content decisions, a slight delusion can be helpful. Research shows that one key to a successful long-term marriage is being *slightly* deluded about how amazing your spouse is.[2] (My spouse must be deluded to stick with me for 20 years, which I'll be the first to say I do not deserve.) The slight but not extreme misperception helps us gloss over minor shortcomings and do the work to stay connected through hardships. In a similar way, if a business has an affinity for some existing content, that business is more likely to care about maintaining and improving it over time.

Sometimes, businesses suffer from the opposite delusion: failure.

Delusions of Content Failure

Occasionally, I come across an organization, or a team within it, that thinks the content situation is much worse than it is. The organization wants to scrap everything and start over. But usually there are strengths and lessons to learn even from content that seems underperforming. For example, in the case of the online retailer I mentioned earlier, we found that the topics covered by the thought leadership actually were the right topics—topics that interested customers and were not covered well by competitors. So the strategy focused on adjusting the tone and substance of the thought leadership, not on starting over from scratch.

Nothing corrects these delusions other than sound analysis of the content situation. I have never seen a content situation that is 100 percent "good" or 100 percent "bad." You will likely see a mix of expected and unexpected strengths and weaknesses.

ALIGN YOUR TEAM AND STAKEHOLDERS BEFORE CHANGE

Whether or not your company is under a delusion, you will be much more likely to unify your content team and stakeholders by starting your content efforts with analysis. Involving your stakeholders in the analysis process and sharing the results gives everyone a common understanding of the current state. When your stakeholders agree on the current state, it will be much easier to engage them to support change later.

SET A "BEFORE" BENCHMARK

Few things persuade people more than a clear comparison of before and after. The evidence is indisputable. The analysis of your current state can give you a number of "before" benchmarks—such as content effectiveness, content operations maturity level, or even the number of content assets— that set the stage for a compelling before and after story. As an example, Scott Rosenberg began a content consolidation effort at Intel in 2015 by documenting the proliferation of content assets, including

- 12,500 Intel.com web pages
- 715 microsites
- 38 mobile apps

This benchmark enabled Rosenberg to document and communicate progress effectively, such as showing the consolidation of 1500 web pages in less than a year.[3] That progress helped him sustain momentum for change at a complex enterprise.

UNCOVER DETAILS FOR REALISTIC IMPLEMENTATION PLANS AND ESTIMATES

When you conduct a thorough analysis, you document items that will not only inform content strategy but also aid in planning the implementation and execution. For example, I find that content assets are a lot like the mogwai in the movie *Gremlins*. If you break the rules about caring for mogwai, they multiply and go rogue. In a similar way, when organizations don't have a strategy and good practices for creating and managing content assets, the content proliferates uncontrollably. Consequently, most organizations have significantly more content than they think they do.

Simply understanding what content you have and its key characteristics, such as its format, goes a long way toward making more accurate estimates for activities such as migrating content into a new platform. There's a meaningful difference between migrating 50,000 assets and 150,000 assets, for instance.

As another example, understanding the quality level of your current content helps you plan to what extent the content needs to change and, consequently, the level of effort needed to change it. There's a meaningful difference in effort between changing the value proposition explained in a product and replacing a product name with the most current name.

BEGIN A SYSTEM OF ONGOING CONTENT INTELLIGENCE SO YOU DON'T HAVE TO DO MOST OF THIS AGAIN

If you're smart about your content analysis approach, then you can use your methodology and data sources to start setting up a system of content intelligence. I explain content intelligence in depth in Section IV, "Prudence: Develop Content Intelligence." My point is that conducting content analysis in many companies involves a significant amount of money as well as setup work and grunt work—especially if content analysis has not been done recently or ever. That work can give you repeatable value in a system of content intelligence. The next time you want an insight about your content, it should take a few hours or days, not weeks.

I hope by now you're convinced why content analysis is important. Now, let's look at how to do it.

HOW TO ANALYZE THE CURRENT STATE

When analyzing your current content situation, focus on the three C's: content, customers (or users), and context (**Figure 4.1**).

Figure 4.1: Analyze your content, customers, and context.

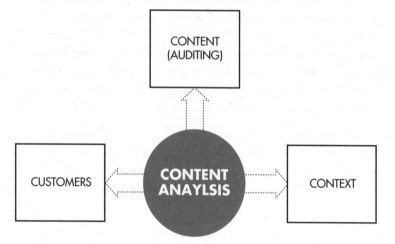

Some people might tell you that a content analysis or audit can take only a few hours[4], especially when they're offering to do it for you. Some people might tell you they have some great swampland in Florida to sell you too. Don't fall for it! I have conducted or overseen hundreds of content analysis efforts. If you have not analyzed your content, customers, or context recently, then expect the effort to take one to three weeks, at least. For large and enterprise companies, expect at least four weeks.

Now that you have a realistic sense of the time involved in this analysis, let's walk through some common ways to analyze each area so you can develop your analysis approach.

CONTENT AUDIT

As you might guess, a content audit is a close look at your existing content. You also might include source material, such as books, brochures, or other material that could be a useful starting point for content on your website and other touchpoints. The content audit starts with a content inventory.

Inventory

The inventory assembles a list and description of the content assets—pages, images, documents, videos, components, and more—that compose your website or digital experiences. You might be able to simply export the inventory from your content management system. More often, especially when you're dealing with large sites or digital experiences, you will need to assemble the inventory from a combination of the following:

- A spidering tool such as CAT (Content Analysis Tool) or ScreamingFrog
- A report from the content management system, digital asset management system, or technology platform
- A report from the analytics tool, such as Google Analytics
- Manual review

You can assemble the inventory in a spreadsheet and track key characteristics of the content, including but not limited to

- Format (such as image or video) or type (such as article or report)
- Topic covered
- Size
- Length, such as character counts
- Metadata, such as titles and tags, currently associated with the assets

Simply completing this inventory is a valuable exercise for most companies to understand the scope and characteristics of their content. Also consider developing a report or dashboard that summarizes your insights (**Figure 4.2**).

Once you have an inventory together, you can audit the content quantitatively and qualitatively.

Quantitative Audit: Content Performance

The most useful quantitative audit, in my experience, is a performance audit. If you're not comfortable with numbers or complex analyses, I recommend having an experienced content or web analyst help you with this audit. To understand performance of the content, assemble analytics into your content inventory. I highlight a few examples in **Table 4.1**.

FINDINGS
Content analysis

The businesses offer different amounts of content for different audiences.
The basic content types and topics align with top user needs.

Amount of content

We reviewed a representative sample of content up to three levels deep in each website's architecture. Respironics by far has the most content, as the sample sizes suggest.

Business website	Content sample size
Respironics	227 modules
HeartStart	172 modules
Lifeline	120 modules
INR (part of RPM)	77 modules
Remote Patient Monitoring (RPM)	40 modules
Telehealth	18 modules

Content types

Respironics and HeartStart have the most variety in content types. The most common content types across all businesses include

- Links / menu / gateway
- Overview
- Promotion / call to action
- Contact information
- Benefits
- Features
- Testimonials

These types align with users' content needs.

Intended audiences

Content targets mostly either a business or consumer audience.

Business audience	Consumer audience
Respironics	Heartstart
Remote Patient Monitoring (RPM)	Lifeline
Telehealth	INR (part of RPM)

Content topics

Compared to other businesses, Respironics has more corporate content, including content for building brand or public relations. Some businesses, such as Lifeline, have brief content about health conditions. Content topics in common across businesses include

- Product / service
- Corporate
- Education / training
- Support / customer service

These topics align with users' content needs.

Figure 4.2: A sample summary of insights from a content inventory

Table 4.1 Content Inventory Analytics

CONTENT PURPOSE OR TYPE	SAMPLE CONTENT PERFORMANCE DATA
Content Marketing Hub/Blog/Magazine	■ Reach: Pageviews and document downloads ■ Engagement: Return visitors and subscribers ■ Engagement: Number of pageviews per session
Sales Content	■ Reach: Pageviews and document downloads ■ Engagement: Return visitors ■ Conversion: Add to cart/purchase/request for information
Support Content	■ Reach: Pageviews and document downloads ■ Engagement: Return visitors ■ Desired conversion: Self-service completion, such as paying a bill online ■ Undesired conversion: Calls or other undesired behavior
Content/Media Product	■ Reach: Pageviews and document downloads ■ Engagement: Return visitors and subscribers ■ Engagement: Number of pageviews per session

Common sources of this quantitative data are your analytics tool, your content management system, and your social media management tool. (In Section IV, you will find more details about data sources that can give you insight into content performance.) After you have the data assembled, you can sort and filter results to determine which content performs well and which doesn't.

In my experience, the results often validate the Pareto principle, or the 80/20 rule. Usually, 20 to 40 percent of the content drives 60 to 80 percent of the performance. At Content Science, we like to work with an organization to identify a threshold of acceptable performance and use that to identify content to consider deleting or retiring. We can also calculate the predicted impact of deleting or retiring that content on performance factors, such as the amount of traffic.

By the end of a performance audit, you will likely have a rather complex spreadsheet that is incredibly useful but not something many stakeholders and executives will review in detail. (Over the past five years, I have encountered more executives who do like seeing these nitty-gritty numbers, so I see this trend changing over the next five years as more companies become data-driven. And you'll be ahead of the trend.) So consider developing a report or dashboard summarizing the audit insights. In **Figure 4.3**, you can see that a small percentage of the content is driving the performance, revealing a number of opportunities to streamline the content.

Figure 4.3: A sample summary of insights from a performance audit

A quantitative inventory and performance audit can give you valuable insight into what content you have and how it's performing. A qualitative audit can complement those insights with more nuances. Let's walk through two useful approaches.

Qualitative Audit: Content Quality
Reviewing the content quality can help shed light on why content performs as it does, how customers perceive it, and whether it meets your company's standards for user experience, brand, accessibility, compliance, and more.

The process is straightforward.

1. Select a content sample.
2. Choose your review criteria.
3. Review the sample or have a content expert review it.
4. If needed, identify areas for additional review.
5. Summarize and share insights.

Select a Sample

Consuming content parallels consuming food, in many ways. Miguel Cervantes wrote in *Don Quixote*, "The proof of the pudding is in the eating. By a small sample we may judge of the whole piece." In the same spirit, if you're dealing with a large set of content, you can gain a tremendous amount of insight about the set by reviewing a sample. Select a representative sample to review. I recommend a 20 percent sample that cuts across *common* examples and *critical* examples (such as content that supports sales for a priority product or service). This sampling rationale is not only intuitive but also grounded in science—specifically, qualitative research methodology.[5]

Furthermore, your quantitative performance audit can inform your sampling choices. For example, you might want to investigate extremely high-performing content to identify potential reasons for its success. You also might want to review extremely low-performing content to understand its potential for improvement or to confirm that it should be deleted or archived.

Choose Review Criteria

The review criteria can be flexible and focus on what is important to you. You can keep it very simple and focus on flagging what content to keep as is, keep and edit, or delete/archive. Or you can add more detail to get more insight. For example, having your content reflect your brand might be critical to your marketing and customer experience strategy. So you might add brand to your criteria and flag which content reflects your brand voice and which does not.

To help you choose your criteria, you also can get a free content quality checklist at the magazine *Content Science Review*: https://review.content-science.com/content-quality-checklist/. This list covers a range of potential criteria to focus on.

Review the Sample and Share Insights

There is nothing quite like a person with content experience taking a close look at the content and putting together observations. A content expert, such as a content strategist, content marketer, or content designer, will see what best practices are applied or missing much more quickly than anyone else.

While the notes for the audit might take form in a spreadsheet, it's also important to summarize and share them. **Figure 4.4**, for example, shows the top opportunities identified from a qualitative audit.

Influence Audit Summary for Mobile Websites

CHARACTERISTIC	PROBLEM OR OPPORTUNITY	EXAMPLE
Meaningful	• Home page branding is overshadowed by large ad for PCR iPhone app *(see example)*. • Promotions to download PCR iPhone app do not articulate meaningful benefits vs the mobile website. Most branded apps are free. • Photos descriptions are basic and do not point out hotel highlights or benefits.	
Relevant	• Promoting the pertinent brand's smartphone app would be more relevant than promoting PCR.	
Credible	• Customers who are not familiar with all of IHG brands are likely to perceive the home page branding as a confusing inconsistency.	
Actionable	• Some error messages would benefit from more instruction to help the customer act appropriately *(see example)*. For example the message at right could say "Check your dates. Your check out cannot be after your check in date." • On the home page, the ad for the PCR application is larger and more prominent than buttons that link to booking or managing a reservation, so it looks like the main action.	

Figure 4.4: A sample summary of insights from a qualitative content audit

Qualitative Audit: Content Automation Potential

As companies face intense pressure to deliver the right content to the right people at the right time 24/7, the smart companies are looking for opportunities to automate content operations. (I explain this trend more in Section V, "Power to Scale: Mature Content Operations.") So for large companies and organizations, I highly recommend reviewing content for opportunities to automate its creation, delivery, or maintenance.

I once oversaw a comprehensive content analysis for a large financial services company. In the course of the audit, we noticed that content describing the products and services was slightly different in different channels/touchpoints, such as the customer website, the advisor website, the whitepapers, the downloadable brochures, and so on. One down side to this situation is that each time the product description changes, it has to be updated manually in all of those channels and touchpoints. Not exactly an efficient process. We pointed out the opportunity to automate the delivery and maintenance of these descriptions. If the financial services company created a single source of those descriptions, those descriptions could be automatically delivered and updated to the channels/touchpoints.

As with reviewing content for quality, reviewing content for automation potential is faster and more accurate when an expert, such as a content strategist or a content engineer, does it. Such experts look for content that

- Is similar but delivered in different places (such as the product and service descriptions just mentioned), which might be an opportunity to consolidate into one version that is reused

- Would benefit from being personalized or being delivered in a personalized way, not unlike Netflix's personalized delivery of content or Amazon's personalized recommendations

- Could be created or edited dynamically, such as creating teasers describing an article from the article title and metadata

I'm only scratching the surface.

Analyzing your content well involves creating an inventory and then assessing the content quantitatively and qualitatively. The insights you gain will take you far in forming your content plans, but that's not all you need. Let's turn to analyzing your customer needs and perceptions.

CUSTOMER NEEDS AND PERCEPTIONS

As we discussed in Chapter 2, your customers (or users or audiences) have needs that they expect your content to address. Your customers also have perceptions about your company, brand, or offerings and your content. Understanding your customers' perspectives will help you

- Further understand why content is performing as it does
- Gain ideas for improving the content to consider in your strategy

Let's walk through three ways to better understand your customers' needs and perceptions related to content.

Updating Customer Journey Maps and Personas

If your company does not already have customer journeys or personas based on solid research, you need them. If you need to create them, I highly recommend these books to help you:

- *Mapping Experiences: A Complete Guide to Creating Value through Journeys, Blueprints, and Diagrams*, by James Kalbach
- *Jobs to Be Done*, by Stephen Wunker, Jessica Wattman, and David Farber
- *Letting Go of the Words: Writing Web Content That Works*, by Janice (Ginny) Redish

Ideally, you will have a customer journey map for each main persona, or customer type. The map in **Figure 4.5** covers the journey for student athletes, an important type of customer for the Rack Athletic Performance Center in Atlanta, Georgia.

To ensure that your customer journey map is useful for content planning, follow these tips to update or enhance them:

- Go beyond customer tasks; add user questions and decisions.

  In the digital world, there is an obsession with customer behavior. Marketers want users to convert. Designers want users to successfully achieve their goals. So it's no surprise that a task (behavior) flow has become a foundation of customer journeys.

  I don't disagree that behavior is important. But I disagree that behavior is everything. Before, during, and after someone takes an action, they

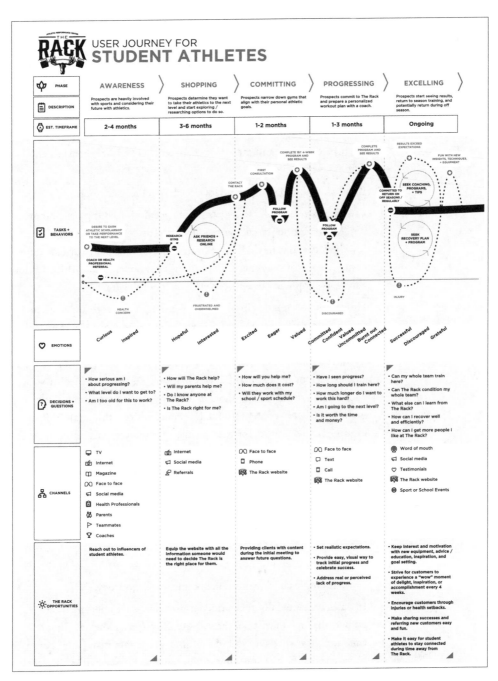

Figure 4.5: Example customer journey map

have thoughts and make decisions. That's an incredible opportunity for content to guide and influence users.

So how do you capture more than behavior in a user journey? Include key questions customers are trying to answer and key decisions they are trying to make. For example, the customer journey for student athletes I shared earlier includes questions such as "Will the Rack work with my schedule? How?" The questions your customers ask will likely be different, and capturing them will help ensure that the content addresses them.

- Build on emotional highs and lows with specific user emotions.

Customers are people, so they experience emotions during their journey. Most commonly, customer journeys represent these as highs and lows, peaks and valleys. That's certainly important. But to be useful for content, user journeys need more specifics about emotion. This addition can be as simple as a brief list in each phase of the journey.

How does this detail help content? By providing clues to appropriate topics, priority, and tone. Imagine you're preparing for a trip from the United States to China and searching online for the vaccinations you need. You find that Centers for Disease Control and Prevention (CDC) suggests a long list of potential vaccinations. You instantly feel anxiety because you're not fond of shots or lengthy visits to the clinic. Now imagine the ways content from CDC could address this anxiety. For example, explore other formats besides a ponderous list and clarify that most travelers to the region need only one or two shots unless they are visiting a rural area or farm. I'm only scratching the surface, of course.

The emotions your customers experience will be different from this travel health example, but the opportunity to let emotions spark ideas for content in each phase of the journey is the same. You will not be able to make the most of that opportunity without identifying specific emotions in your user' journeys.

- Track multiple channels or touchpoints for the journey.

In our fragmented digital world, our users and customers interact with us through more than the website. If your user journeys ignore this fact, they will have limited usefulness for content and might even cause confusion. The spinning studio Burn, as I described in Chapter 2, uses touchpoints ranging from the website to kiosks to digital signage to emails.

When you know the channels your users prefer or could use in each stage, you can identify more easily opportunities to

- Reuse content across channels.

- Optimize content for priority channels.

- Distribute content more effectively in each journey stage.

Let's consider an example. A media company focused on the US automobile industry decided it wanted to better support the customer journey for buying vehicles. The company identified the earliest stage as Dream and reviewed its own user research as well as current trends for how millennials in the United States become inspired about vehicles. The company realized that visually oriented social media channels such as Pinterest and Instagram were crucial to supporting the Dream stage. With that clear awareness, the media company could flesh out the content strategy and social media strategy for that stage.

Don't leave your customer journeys open to the risk of being pretty but impractical. Use these tips to make them useful for content planning.

Content Mapping

When you have a solid understanding of your customers' journeys and the existing content (or source material), you can map your existing content to those journeys. This process will help you see

- Where your existing content meets customer needs or could meet those needs with minor changes

- Gaps between customer needs and your existing content

- Overlaps or redundancies in your content, such as having too much content to address one customer need or touchpoint

You can do this mapping yourself, as an individual. Or you can turn it into a group activity with your team or stakeholders. When you make content mapping a group activity, you engage the group early in understanding the current state of your content. Instead of reporting to them, you involve them in the process of discovering the current state, which can be much more compelling than a report.

If you decide to make content mapping a group activity, I suggest take the following steps:

1. Print a list of the content. If you have a lot of content, you can group it into categories (such as troubleshooting articles), or conduct a series of group activities until you have included all of the content.

2. Set up a whiteboard or easel pad with the major stages of the customer journey.

3. Provide group participants with a copy of the content list, sticky notes, and markers.

4. Have participants work together to write an item from the list on a sticky note, and then place it on the whiteboard or easel pad. If you have many participants, you can have them work in groups of three or four. (See **Figure 4.6**.)

5. After participants finish mapping the content, lead a discussion about the gaps, overlaps, and the content that does not seem to fit at all.

Figure 4.6: A group collaborates to map content to a customer journey.

Assessing Content Effectiveness

An analysis area that I've developed with the Content Science team is content effectiveness, or how effectively your customers perceive the content. I am enthusiastic about how this analysis sheds more light on why and how content performs as it does with your customers. We developed this assessment out of our studies of content credibility and trust, where we focused heavily on how people perceive content.

Why do I care so much about customers' perceptions of content? Because, to paraphrase the adage, your customers' perceptions are your reality. Your customers' perceptions, colored by their beliefs, emotions, education, and more, drive their behavior. You cannot change their behavior, such as persuading them to use your self-service content, without managing or influencing their perceptions. Your biggest opportunity to do so is content.

In our research, we identified six elements of content effectiveness (**Table 4.2**), and these elements have held up over the course of collecting data from more than 150,000 people.

Table 4.2 The Six Elements of Content Effectiveness

CATEGORY	QUESTION
Discoverability/Findability	Does the content seem easy to find?
Polish	Does the content format and style seem to be high quality?
Accuracy	Does the content seem correct and up to date?
Usefulness	Does the content seem useful or helpful?
Relevance/Meaning	Does the content seem relevant and meaningful?
Influence/Persuasion	Does the content aid in completing a goal or making a decision?

The Content Science team developed a tool called ContentWRX to help automate this assessment, from collecting data to creating a content effectiveness score. You can also conduct this assessment by assembling and reviewing the following types of data:

- **Voice of customer data:** Mentions of content in survey or poll responses; comments on your content; email and chat inquiries; phone call inquiries

- **Social listening:** Mentions of content in social media and online forums

- **Microanalytics:** Understanding where people linger, click, save, copy, and more to help explain their reactions to content (**Figure 4.7**)

Figure 4.7: National Cancer Institute assesses the effectiveness of content on cancer.gov.

Understanding your customers' needs and perspective will complement your content analysis. You also will benefit from considering the context surrounding your content and customers.

CONTEXT

As a retired US Army general and the former Chairman of the Joint Chiefs of Staff, Martin Dempsey is no stranger to developing and executing strategy. He once observed, "Strategy is, at some level, the ability to predict what's going to happen, but it's also about understanding the context in which it is being formulated." I could not agree more. Let's turn to four contextual factors that will be important to consider in your content strategy.

Content Maturity

This area focuses on what happens "behind the scenes" with your content. After encountering company after company with unrealistic expectations of their content capacity, the Content Science team and I developed a set of content maturity models. I'm sharing our simplest and most widely applicable model in **Figure 4.8**.

Content Maturity Checklist ™

Where are you now? Where do you want to be?

CONTENT MATURITY LEVEL		INDICATORS
1 Piloting	☐ ☐	1. Have you successfully launched a small content effort? 2. Are you seeing results, such as a boost in sales or sales leads, from your small content effort?
2 Scaling	☐ ☐ ☐	1. Are you developing a broader vision for content at your organization? 2. Have you won more budget to invest in content efforts? 3. Are you applying lessons learned from your piloting phase to other brands, channels, products, teams, or areas of the customer experience?
3 Sustaining	☐ ☐ ☐	1. Are you investigating how marketing and content automation can make your approach more efficient? 2. Are you establishing content guidelines and tools to make your content approach easy and efficient to repeat? 3. Are you developing a plan to evaluate your content approach in terms of big goals and small indicators that you're progressing toward those goals?
4 Thriving	☐ ☐ ☐	1. Is your approach to sustaining running smoothly, so you're free to experiment with new content approaches, formats, and techniques? 2. Do your teams have the right processes and technology in place to support agility? Can they respond to problems, such as customer concerns, and opportunities, such as tweeting a clever response during the Super Bowl, quickly? 3. Is your evaluation showing progress toward your goals or achievement of your goals? Are you seeing boosts to your reputation, earned media, sales or sales leads, and customer satisfaction?

My Current Level: _____   My Target Next Level: _____

Figure 4.8: A sample content maturity model

If you find that your company is at a low level of maturity, take heart in the fact you're not alone. In the Content Operations and Leadership Study, 70.9% of participants reported being at the lower scaling level. It's not too late to catch up or get ahead.

Assessing content maturity is another opportunity to involve your team or stakeholders. You can conduct a survey or a workshop activity that asks your stakeholders about their impressions of the current approach to content operations (**Figure 4.9**).

Figure 4.9: A group collaborates to assess content maturity.

Brand and Reputation

This area focuses on the broader perceptions that customers and potential customers have about your company and its reputation. When you have a realistic understanding of those perceptions, you can develop a content strategy that sustains or changes the perceptions. GE, for example, has credited the significant improvement in perceptions of its reputation in 2015 to its content efforts.[6]

Your marketing leadership might already have a system in place to track these perceptions. If not, then you can conduct a survey or poll as well as mine your voice of customer and social listening data.

Technology Trends and Business Dynamics

As the words "technology trends and business dynamics" imply, what you consider here will change as technology and business trends evolve. For the near future, you will want to consider how advances in technology, such as machine learning and artificial intelligence, can realistically help you. Content or business ambitions that might have seemed out of reach in the past, such as personalization and automation, are much more feasible now.

Content Landscape

The content landscape is other sources of content that your customers use or are exposed to in the course of their journeys. These content sources might be your business competitors, or they might not be. For example, the online retailer mentioned previously created thought leadership about niche health conditions and topics such as plantar fasciitis and heel pain. The retailer's competition for this content was not other retailers but other sources of health content, such as WebMD, Cleveland Clinic, Sharecare, and Mayo Clinic. Identify the potential content sources that your customers are likely to encounter in their journeys.

You'll learn more about understanding and using insights about the content landscape in the next chapter, "Play to Win."

PROMISING TOOLS

In this chapter, I have mentioned a few tools that can help you analyze your content, customers, and context. A number of other tools can help you conduct analysis and establish a system of ongoing intelligence. You can find a complete list of these tools in Section V. Additionally, we maintain a list of these tools at content-science.com.

With a thorough analysis of your current state complete, you are ready to put together a strategy and a set of plans to change your current state into your desired future state. Let's start making your company's content vision a reality.

REFERENCES

1 "Content Operations and Leadership Study: Full Report," https://content-science.com/professional-services/capabilities/content-operations-study/

2 "Are Deluded People More Fun? Barking Up the Wrong Tree," www.bakadesuyo.com/2012/07/are-deluded-people-more-fun/

3 "Intel Addresses Modern Marketing Challenges through Digital Governance," *Content Science Review* https://review.content-science.com/2016/10/intel-addresses-modern-marketing-challenges-through-digital-governance/

4 "How to Do a Content Audit in a Few Hours," Content Marketing Institute http://contentmarketinginstitute.com/2018/02/content-audit-hours/

5 "Qualitative Research Guidelines Project," Robert Wood Johnson Foundation www.qualres.org/

6 "How GE's Katrina Craigwell Uses Marketing to Build Positive Experiences," American Marketing Association www.ama.org/publications/MarketingNews/Pages/shes-blinding-them-with-science.aspx

5 PLAY TO WIN

· ·

Synthesize your analysis and vision into a winning content strategy.

STRATEGY IS THE STARTING POINT FOR A TRANSFORMATION THAT
NEEDS TO OCCUR AND HOW THAT COMPANY MUST CHANGE TO WIN.

—Lynne Doughtie

I SUGGEST A NEW STRATEGY, R2: LET THE WOOKIEE WIN.

—C3PO

In Chapter 4, we reviewed how to conduct an analysis to inform your content strategy. By now you might wonder, "So what does all this information mean for my content?" We'll answer that question and more in this chapter. To start, let's talk about what content strategy isn't.

CONTENT SKILLS + BEST PRACTICES ≠ CONTENT STRATEGY

I'm a big fan of tennis, a sport that has existed in some form since 1873. I love watching it, and I really love playing it. One reason tennis has enthralled me for many (many) years is the interplay of skills and best practices with strategy. You have to have certain skills and know certain best practices to play tennis. If you can't use a racquet to hit that fuzzy yellow ball over the net and within the court lines repeatedly, you'll never win a tennis match. Knowing best practices based on decades of experience helps too. You can select from high-percentage shots—shots that tend to work most of the time, such as a deep cross-court forehand with topspin—and risky, low-percentage shots, such as the drop shot or a low shot down the line. These skills and knowledge can take you far in a tennis match. And if you're playing against someone with far fewer skills and less knowledge, you might even win. (There's no question Serena Williams would beat me on skill alone.) But to win against an opponent with comparable or better skills and knowledge, you need something else. You need strategy.

In the same way, you can acquire a range of content skills and knowledge, from basic to advanced. You can use plain language and format your text to be easy to scan, for instance. But so can every other business or organization. To win, content best practices are not enough. You need content strategy.

So where does strategy come from? In tennis, your strategy for a match evolves partly from an understanding of your strengths and your competitor's weaknesses. Tennis star Colleen "Coco" Vandeweghe, for example, serves exceptionally well and can usually count on that strength to win most of her service games. That strength, in turn, frees her to take more risks on aggressive point-winning shots during games in which her opponent is serving. And when she plays an opponent who likes to get in a rhythm of long rallies and hates the stop-and-start of short points, Coco's strategy often becomes even more effective.

The same consideration of your strengths often goes for content strategy. Let's take the online retailer I mentioned in Chapter 4. This retailer sold comfort shoes and a wide range of injury prevention, treatment, and pain-management products for feet and legs—heel cushions, braces, arch supports, and more. In other words, the retailer had defined a clear niche. This niche acted as a content strength for the retailer. As you might expect, no other retailers offered much content about foot and lower-body diseases, injuries, and conditions. As you might *not* expect, neither do major health information sites such as WebMD, Mayo Clinic, and Cleveland Clinic. So the niche retailer built a repository of useful, engaging content—articles, quizzes, slides, and more—about these foot and lower-body health issues in partnership with the Podiatry Institute. And soon the niche retailer "beat" other retailers and health information sites in visibility in search engine rankings, which grew the retailer's organic traffic by 200 percent within a year and grew its weekly sales by 36 percent.

Hopefully you are starting to see the difference between applying content best practices and building a content strategy. Let's talk more about building a winning content strategy.

HOW TO DEVELOP A WINNING CONTENT STRATEGY

If you haven't realized that I'm an odd bird yet, this will clinch it for you: I'm addicted to business strategy books. I have read or listened to dozens and dozens of them. Most have offered useful insights, tips, or guidance (hence my addiction). But one book stands out among them: *Playing to Win*. In this *Wall Street Journal* bestseller, Procter & Gamble CEO A.G. Lafley and his strategy advisor Roger Martin offer an approach and myriad examples that show "how strategy really works." The duo also offer a set of questions so valuable that I have adapted and expanded them to apply to content. Use these questions as a foundation for your content strategy.

ITERATE BETWEEN ANSWERING THESE FIVE KEY QUESTIONS

Fundamentally, your content strategy comes down to addressing five main questions (**Figure 5.1**).

Notice the arrows leading to and from each question? Those arrows reflect how answering these questions really works. You will likely answer some, think about the consequences, change your answers, and then change the answers that depend on those previous answers, and... you get the idea. The answers to these questions are interrelated, so iterating your answers is normal, even good.

Let's walk through these core questions and important supporting questions so that you can start to use them.

What Is Our Winning Aspiration?

This answer should factor in your content vision, as we discussed in Chapter 3, and your business goals. For example, the foot health retailer I mentioned aspired to be the go-to lower-body health outfitter, or the REI of lower-body health. This aspiration crystallized the retailer's desire to be a trusted advisor and to increase sales responsibly.

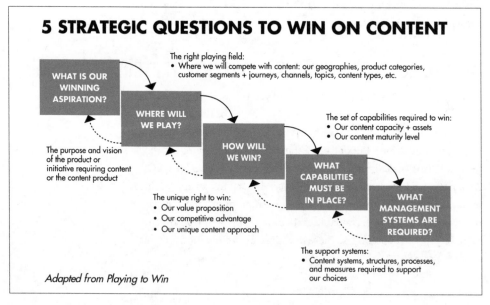

Figure 5.1: Five key content strategy questions

Where Will We Play?

This question drives you to consider the right playing field—the place to compete where you have the best chance to win. As our world becomes increasingly digital and our relationships with customers grow longer, we face many potential places to make a content play. We can play in myriad channels, touchpoints, and formats, such as our website, in mobile applications, on social media sites, in print, on kiosks and digital signage, in voice applications such as Alexa, in games and virtual reality, and many more. We also have the opportunity to play in many stages or phases of the customer relationship, as we talked about in Chapter 4. While it might be tempting to compete on all of these "fields," the reality is that you will have to be selective. Even Serena Williams does not play in every professional tennis tournament. And even Amazon still does not make a big play in content to educate customers before and after a sale—the kind of content our successful foot health retailer developed.

The analysis you do, as explained in Chapter 4, will go a long way toward informing your answer to this question and the questions that follow. Additionally, as you start to answer the following questions, you will realize quickly why you have to carefully select where to play.

How Will We Win?

Another way of thinking about this question is "What gives us the unique right to win?" Answering this question should consider and potentially synthesize your value proposition, your competitive advantage, and your unique content approach. For example, most companies and organizations have a tremendous amount of expertise in a number of subjects. A medical technology company cannot operate without expertise in both medicine and technology, for example. That expertise is a potential competitive advantage, enabling a company to create more credible, specialized, or unique content.

As another example, Tennessee Valley Authority (TVA) has accumulated since its founding, in 1933, a wealth of visual content assets, from photographs to videos to diagrams, that most companies and organizations do not come close to possessing. TVA has embraced using these visual assets to tell unique educational stories about their energy plants, their approach to environmental stewardship, their involvement in economic development, and much more (**Figure 5.2**).

Figure 5.2: Tennessee Valley Authority possesses a unique repository of visual content assets.

As a different example, FitBit has a special relationship with its customers that is mediated by unique touchpoints, such as its watch and mobile application. FitBit can take advantage of what I call "coachable moments"— where a customer has succeeded, failed, or hit a significant milestone toward a health goal—with content. And FitBit does. FitBit provides immediate messages to address the moment and guides customers to more in-depth advice and guidance (**Figure 5.3**).

Figure 5.3: FitBit takes advantage of coachable moments in its unique relationship and touchpoints with customers.

As you consider your unique right to win on content, review your analysis and look for indicators of your unique

- Expertise
- Brand values, characteristics, or personality
- Existing content assets
- Relationship and touchpoints with customers
- Gaps in competitive content offerings

Additionally, remember that in content your competitors are not only your business competitors but also potential sources of pertinent content. For example, the niche foot retailer was competing not only with other online shoe stores but also with other sources of health content. FitBit competes not only with other fitness watches but also with other sources of fitness, wellness, and performance content, such as Under Armour's myFitnessPal.

Now let's turn to questions about making the content strategy happen.

What Capabilities Must Be in Place?

Just as Serena Williams could not build a match strategy around a serve if she did not have the ability to serve exceptionally well, so you cannot build a content strategy without having the related content capabilities. This question turns attention to your content capacity and maturity level and even more attention to your content assets. And if you have gaps in your capabilities, the question becomes "Are we willing to close these gaps so we can execute our strategy? Or do we need to adjust our strategy to account for these gaps?"

For instance, companies ranging from Red Bull to TD Ameritrade have created in-house studios that give them the ability to offer rich editorial and educational content. Other companies taking this path include Marriott, American Express, and REI. If your company is not willing to make that kind of commitment, then you need to closely consider how you will adjust and adapt existing capabilities to achieve your strategy. For example, I worked with a credit monitoring company on developing a robust content strategy for consumers. We discovered that even though the company had little content capability in the consumer side (B2C) of the business, the business side (B2B) of the company possessed some useful capabilities. As a result, we explored how to use those capabilities in support of the consumer content strategy.

What Management or Operational Systems Are Required?

This question goes further into sustaining your content strategy. Consider what content management technology, management processes, and measures you have or will need. For example, we worked with a telecommunications and entertainment conglomerate on a personalization-driven content strategy, such as providing highly relevant offers and content suggestions. In the course of fleshing out the strategy, we discovered that even though the company possessed a wealth of customer data and a new, robust content management system, their systems lacked integration and alignment. At the same time, their content was not structured in their content management system at the right level of granularity. The content was mostly composed of pages and documents, not of components (or chunks) that could be extracted and reused. The telecommunications and entertainment company realized they had to fix these systems before they could embrace the content strategy they desired. (For more about changing your systems, see Section V.)

In addition to considering how your systems will need to change to support your content strategy, start to think about how you will measure the success of your content strategy. I discuss measures more in depth in Chapters 8 through 11, but the sooner you explore potential ways to measure the impact of your content strategy, the better.

When you have answers that you and your team or stakeholders are comfortable with, you can move forward with your content strategy. Or you can explore options and test concepts to further refine your content strategy.

EXPLORE OPTIONS AND TEST CONCEPTS

A content strategy can seem abstract and, consequently, lend itself to wide interpretation. What does being the REI of lower-body health really mean, for example? Before you commit to a content strategy, you can develop concepts that illustrate different options, and then test those options with your customers or users. For example, we worked with the niche foot health retailer to test options that represented differences such as voice, style, topics, layout, product merchandising, and more. The feedback we gained helped the retailer confirm that the content strategy was likely to succeed and refine the strategy. For example, the testing revealed an overwhelming preference for a friendly and accessible voice (**Figure 5.4**).

Figure 5.4: A foot health retailer tested options before fully committing to a content strategy.

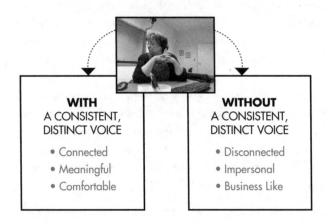

HOW USERS DESCRIBED CONTENT

WITH A CONSISTENT, DISTINCT VOICE	**WITHOUT** A CONSISTENT, DISTINCT VOICE
• Connected • Meaningful • Comfortable	• Disconnected • Impersonal • Business Like

TWO TIPS FOR LARGE ORGANIZATIONS

I've worked with large private and public companies, including six of the Fortune 50. In my experience, the following two tips can help as you work to define content strategy.

You Need More Than One Content Strategy

With every business function going digital, you likely need a content strategy for each function, such as marketing and support. The exact combination of content strategies you need will vary from organization to organization, but the need for more than one content strategy is the same. You can start by picking a function or experience to develop a content strategy using Chapters 3 through 5. And then you can repeat the approach in other areas.

Content Strategies Work Best When Aligned and Unified by a Content Vision

People who love to "geek out" on content sometimes talk about a unified content strategy. Most people who say this are referring to reusing content in multiple channels or touchpoints. I find that content reuse is a valuable tactic, but it alone is not a strategy. I also find that a single content strategy for an enterprise does not make a sense (see the previous tip). However,

I *do* find that a large company benefits from a vision that unifies the content strategies. For example, I recently worked with a credit monitoring company that viewed content as critical to transforming the experience the company gave consumers. We developed a set of five content strategies unified by a core content vision, as you can see summarized in **Figure 5.5**. This vision has helped people involved in the different content strategies understand how their effort fits into the overall consumer content vision.

CONTENT VISION FOR CONSUMER CREDIT HEALTH

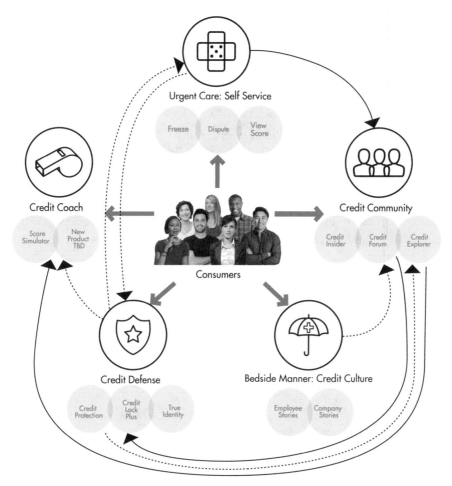

Figure 5.5: A sample content vision that unifies consumer content strategies under the vision of credit health

TWO TIPS FOR SMALL AND MEDIUM ORGANIZATIONS

If you work for a small business or organization, keep these tips in mind.

Your Size and Focus Is an Advantage

You might be tempted to think that you can't compete, especially against organizations larger than yours. Think again. Skim the tips I just shared for large companies. If it sounds like big organizations have much to coordinate, that's because they do. Making a simple editorial decision might take three weeks for them and one day for you. Large companies are often slow and sprawling in their approach to content. If you can be nimble and focus on your niche the way the spinning studio Burn and the foot health retailer did, you will have a significant advantage over any competitor.

Your Lack of Resources Makes Content Strategy Even More Critical

You do not have money to burn, so use the money you have wisely. Define and test the content strategy before you create, buy, or curate content assets. For example, we helped the Rack Athletic Performance Center, a small business in Atlanta, crystallize its content niche, especially topics and formats, so that a variety of its employees could contribute supporting content, such as articles or workshops, efficiently (**Figure 5.6**).

Once you have a potentially winning content strategy, what's next? One important step is planning to offer effective and influential content. In Section III, we explore how to make the content supporting your strategy as compelling as possible.

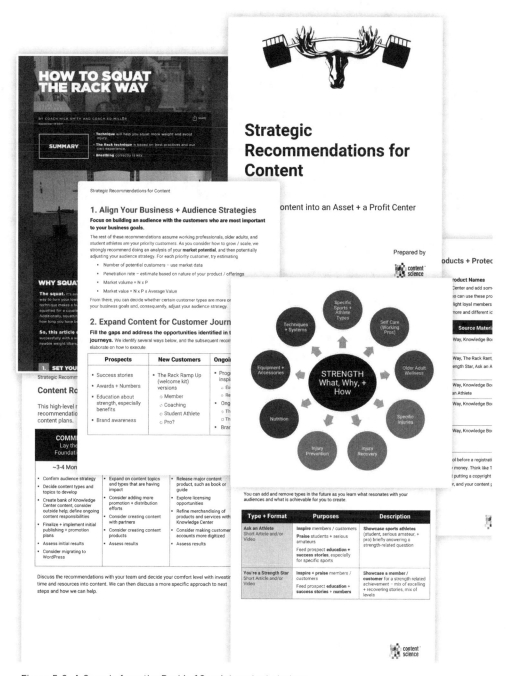

Figure 5.6: A Sample from the Rack's 10-point content strategy

PERSUASION: OFFER EFFECTIVE AND INFLUENTIAL CONTENT

· ·

• •

Make your content make a difference for your customers.

6 MAKE YOUR CONTENT EFFECTIVE

• •

Does your content work for your customers?

I LEARNED EARLY IN SPORTS THAT TO BE EFFECTIVE—FOR A PLAYER
TO PLAY THE BEST HE CAN PLAY—IS A MATTER OF CONCENTRATION
AND BEING UNAWARE OF DISTRACTIONS, POSITIVE OR NEGATIVE.

—Tom Landry

STAY ON TARGET.

—Gold Five, *Star Wars*

If you read the first edition of this book, you know that I'm fascinated by persuasion and its related fields, including psychology, communication, and rhetoric. (If you didn't, now you know!) This fascination stems from the many, many times in my life where I felt I failed to persuade, and the few times I felt I was successful.

One of those few early times in my life occurred in fifth grade. My teacher, Mrs. Hoerter, had a point system to encourage positive behavior. If she gave you points on a particular day, you felt as if you'd conquered the world. Five additional points was the max, and the words "plus five!" were magic to my and my classmates' ears. If she neither gave nor took away points, that was normal. If she took away points, especially five points, that was devastating. To be honest, I don't even remember what we could do with the points. But I remember I really wanted to gain points and never lose them.

So one day I was working on an assignment, and a few classmates nearby got into a bit of an argument. They started to raise their voices. Big mistake. Mrs. Hoerter, who was working with students on the other side of the room, looked in our direction and said loudly "minus five!" Horrors! I consoled myself by thinking that Mrs. Hoerter knew I wasn't part of the commotion and didn't mean me. But that afternoon I looked at my point chart and saw in black ink the dreaded minus 5. What to do!?

I immediately thought about our recent English lesson, where we learned about writing a persuasive essay. And I decided the next day to write Mrs. Hoerter a letter explaining why I did not deserve the dreaded minus five, trying to use techniques from the lesson, such as giving three reasons and explaining them clearly. Before I left the room for the afternoon school bus, I put the letter in an envelope I had brought from home and then left the envelope on Mrs. Hoerter's chair. The next morning I walked to my desk, and lo and behold, an envelope with my name in Mrs. Hoerter's hand-writing was waiting. I nervously opened it, and to my great relief, she had agreed to restore those five points. That English lesson worked!

So it's safe to say that when I explore persuasion I indulge in some "me-search." The good news for you is that in my quest to learn more about persuasion, I have accumulated a variety of facts, principles, and examples that you might find useful. In this chapter, we address the essentials to make content effective. It's tough to be influential through content without these essentials.

AN OVERVIEW OF CONTENT EFFECTIVENESS

I consider the dimensions identified in **Table 6.1** and mentioned in Chapter 4 to be essential to effective content.

Table 6.1 Dimensions of Content Effectiveness

DIMENSION	DESCRIPTION
Discoverability/Findability	The content is easy for customers to find and consume.
Polish	Customers perceive the content format and style as appropriately polished.
Accuracy	Customers perceive the content as correct or up to date.
Usefulness	Customers perceive the content as useful or helpful.
Relevance/Meaning	Customers perceive the content as relevant or meaningful.

In the case of my fifth-grade letter, I made it easy for Mrs. Hoerter to find by placing it on her chair. My letter was not a slick brochure or video, but it was much more polished than, say, yelling or crying. I made a painstaking effort to state the facts accurately, not exaggerate them. I wrote the letter soon after the dreaded minus five happened, so the letter was highly relevant. And I tried to lay out the information Mrs. Hoerter would need to make the decision whether to restore those five precious points. Without these essentials in place, I likely would not have had the opportunity to influence my teacher. In a similar way, your company will have a tough time earning the opportunity to influence your customers without making your content effective.

Are all of these dimensions of content effectiveness really necessary? I've wondered that myself. Luckily, the Content Science team has some data to help us get answers—data collected by our ContentWRX software from more than 100,000 content users about these dimensions of content effectiveness. We analyzed this data to explore the relationship between the dimensions and not only confirmed their importance but also learned more about why they're important. Let's walk through the dimensions in more detail.

DISCOVERABILITY/FINDABILITY

Make your content easy for customers to find and consume—in both reality and *perception*.

WHY IT MATTERS

The obvious reason why discoverability and findability matter is that if customers can't find your content, it might as well not exist. Today, making your organization's content easy to find or discover usually takes work, thanks in part to the amount of content and data on the internet doubling roughly every five years.

A not-so-obvious reason? Our research using the ContentWRX data revealed a surprising impact of content findability. If your customers have difficulty finding your content, that experience distorts their perspective on the content itself. Let's look at some proof. In **Figure 6.1**, you can see that people who reported that content was easy to find were significantly more likely to report that it was accurate, relevant, and useful than were people who experienced difficulty (but eventually found the content they needed).

Another way of looking at this insight is that if your customers had trouble finding your content but eventually did, they are

- Less than half as likely to view that content as accurate
- Nearly one-third as likely to view that content as relevant
- Less than half as likely to perceive that content as helpful to accomplishing their goal

You could offer the most amazing content ever produced, but it will not matter if customers experience difficulty finding it. Content findability is the first impression you make on your customers, and the stakes for that impression are very high. I regret I have experienced this phenomenon first hand. Last year, my company launched an online academy. (Creatively named Content Science Academy.) In our eagerness to share the academy with the world, we allowed people to sign up for a few experimental courses that were in a format not quite ready for primetime. Consequently, customers had difficulty accessing and using the experimental courses and complained. But even though the course material was well received in other training formats, these customers also criticized the material. Ouch. The bad first impression of difficult-to-access course material distorted our customers' perceptions of the material and the rest of the experience. Instead of winning over fans for our innovative new academy, we discouraged them from using it again.

EFFECT OF CONTENT FINDABILITY ON PERCEPTION

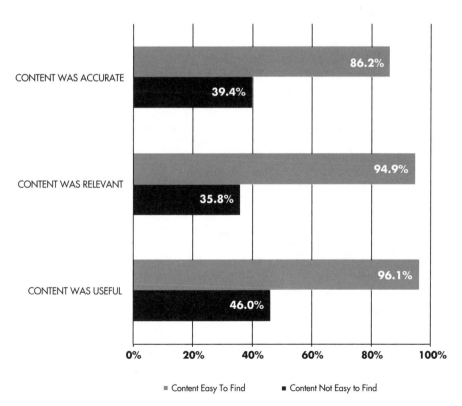

Figure 6.1: People perceive content that is hard to find (but eventually found) as less accurate, relevant, and useful than easy-to-find content

How can you avoid my mistake and connect your customers with your content? Let's turn to a few tips.

TOP TIPS

It's time to modernize your company's approach to content findability with a mix of new thinking and old-hat best practices.

Bring the Content to the Customer Through Personalization

Is it realistic to always put the burden on your customers, users, or audiences to find your content? When your customers get to your website, mobile application, or other digital touchpoint, are they really willing to wade through multiple levels of navigation or a set of search filters and settings so complex they look like a control center in a spaceship? Start thinking about how your company can take on the burden of connecting your customers with the right content. One of the most effective ways to do so is to embrace personalization.

Whenever I speak about personalization at a conference or corporate training, I ask attendees to name a great example. Amazon is usually on the tip of their tongues. It's not hard to understand why, with the many ways Amazon connects customers to the most pertinent products possible. In a similar spirit, think about how to Amazon-ify your content, such as

- Proactively offering your customers suggested content or information immediately when they visit your site
- Showing your customers or users which content that people with similar interests or needs found useful
- Giving your customers suggestions for content similar to the content they just consumed
- Reminding or alerting customers of important decisions, tasks, and more
- Customizing offers or messages based on your customers' interests or status
- Planning microcopy and contextual help to guide customers in the moment rather than making them search for instructions

You can bring the content when users expect or demand it… or when it will surprise and delight them. Take the Weather Channel, for example. When a hurricane, a snowstorm, or other extreme weather looms, people check the Weather Channel website and mobile application. What about sunny days? Not so much. So the Weather Channel decided to delight and engage their mobile application users by delivering clever, personalized content for more types of weather and for weather holidays, like the countdown to an eclipse. The result? Content strategist Lindsey Howard notes

> Since launching, we increased performance in double digits across all priority metrics, including visits per user, sponsorship traffic, total impressions, and retention. This is particularly significant in an app world where every percentage point counts. International engagement, a key factor in global relevance and expansion, skyrocketed. A priority metric for content strategy, click-through rate, went up 23 percent in less than three months.[1]

Personalizing content delivery requires content intelligence as well as content engineering. We'll talk more about what these disciplines are and how you can take advantage of them in Sections IV and V.

Apply Solid Web Search Engine and Social Media Optimization Best Practices

I don't mean the SEO snake oil mentioned in Chapter 1. I mean tried-and-true practices that will help search engines, such as Google and the search engines on your website or mobile app, retrieve the right content. These practices are my top picks:

- Focus on topics your customers care about.
- When possible, don't focus on exactly the same topics as your competitors. Tools such as Google AdWords and Moz can help you assess your options.
- Use the topic and topic phrases in page names, asset names, metadata descriptions, and text content.
- Use a tool such as Moz or a search engine optimization plug-in to help automate and check search engine optimization (Drupal and WordPress have several, for example).

- For web pages, specify an image that will display when the page is shared on social media. Adjusting your web page administration template or adding a plug-in can enable this feature if you do not already have it.

Start Engineering Your Content for Retrieval by Voice Interfaces, ChatBots, and Similar Emerging Touchpoints

The future is quickly becoming now. We'll talk more about this content engineering in Sections V and VI.

Archive Outdated and Underperforming Content

This best practice in content maintenance is more important than ever. And too many companies and organizations are still not following it. So it bears repeating: Get rid of outdated and underperforming content. Doing so is now critical to making the rest of your organization's content findable. Let me explain.

If your company continues to clog its digital presence with content that no longer works, your company

- Reduces the chances that your customers will discover the most appropriate content. You're making your customers look for a needle in a haystack.
- Risks that you will cannibalize the search engine optimization of your new or current content with outdated content about similar topics.

I encourage you to view maintaining current content as a must-happen best practice, or your company's investment in content will not matter. It's like trying to improve your health with a fancy gym, expensive personal trainer, and nifty equipment—without trimming excessive junk food from your diet. The junk food habit undermines the hard work you do at the gym, not to mention that it wastes your time and money.

If maintaining content does not sound particularly easy or fun to you, you are not alone. But in Sections IV and V, we'll talk more about how establishing and even automating good content habits in your content operations can help.

Let's move on to two more dimensions of content effectiveness, polish and accuracy.

POLISH AND ACCURACY

Offer up-to-date and correct content at an appropriate level of polish or production quality.

WHY IT MATTERS

In the same study of ContentWRX data, we discovered that if people perceive content as accurate and polished, they are significantly more likely to perceive it as relevant and useful. If your customers are not confident in your facts, wonder whether your information is current, or trip over frequent typos or display glitches, they will have difficulty taking your content seriously. Even worse, your customers will have trouble meeting their goals. **Figure 6.2** shows that people who perceive content as accurate are five times as likely to report completing their goals as people who do not and are twice as likely to report completing their goals as people who are not sure of the accuracy.

RESPONDENTS WHO COMPLETED THEIR GOAL

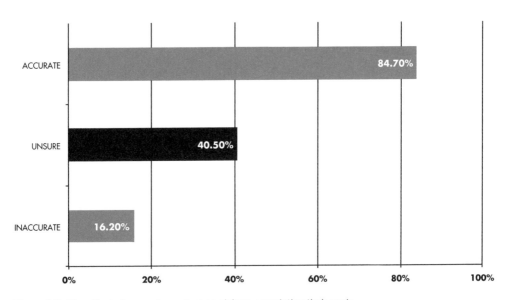

Figure 6.2: The effect of accurate content on visitors completing their goals

Offering polished and clearly accurate content is not as easy as it sounds. So let's turn to a few tips that can help you sustain accurate and polished content.

TOP TIPS

These tips help address the reality of your content's accuracy and polish as well as your customers' perceptions.

Archive or Update Outdated Content

Yes, we did just discuss outdated content as a findability problem. It's also an accuracy problem. If your company doesn't archive or update outdated content, then your company will not only experience findability problems but also risk the following:

- Your customers mistakenly using content that is inaccurate, which can lead to confusion, unrealistic expectations, and serious errors—all of which can lead to returned purchases, customer churn, lawsuits, and lost trust.

- Looking like one of those organizations that doesn't care. The outdated content might not cause a major disaster, but it immediately undermines your customers' confidence and trust in you. If you can't keep your content current, why should customers believe you can handle their business or advise them on high-stakes topics such as health?

Let's look at an example in *AutoTrader*. This bumblebee Camaro classified ad (**Figure 6.3**) graced the internet in 2011, so it is full of now-outdated references, such as the *Transformers* movie. More importantly, this Camaro is no longer really for sale. This ancient classified ad is customer frustration waiting to happen, not to mention a turnoff for potential readers of Auto-Trader editorial content.

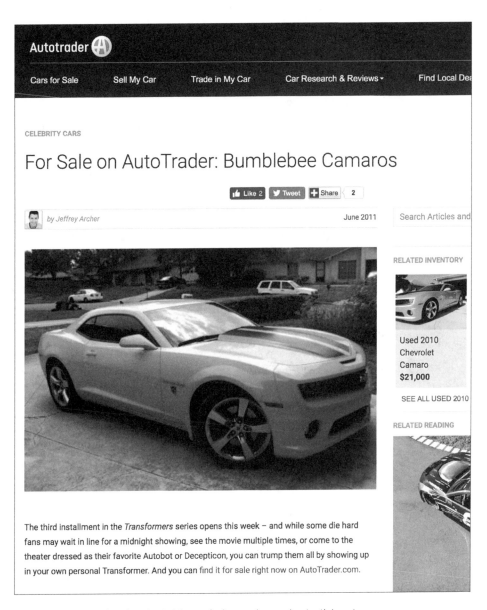

Figure 6.3: This outdated content risks confusing readers and potential customers.

Give Customers Strong Cues That Content Is Accurate

Don't be shy about letting your customers know that the content is current and grounded in facts or evidence. If your customers do not perceive your content as accurate, it might as well not be. A few ways to give your customers confidence include

- Providing dates that the content was published, reviewed, or updated
- Specifying clearly the product or plan version discussed in the content
- Citing and potentially linking to credible sources of facts or statistics
- Specifying how long the content, such as recommendations or guidelines or warnings, applies
- Ensuring that links to more or supporting information are current

The guiding principle here is to tell people that your content is accurate and why.

Ensure the Content Is Usable and Accessible in the Right Channels or Touchpoints

The minimum level of polish your content must have is usability. Web content must be layered, chunked, and labeled, for example. Videos must have transcripts or closed captioning. Fortunately, several resources already cover this ground well.

- *Letting Go of the Words* by Ginny Redish
- *Don't Make Me Think* by Steve Krug
- *Rocket Surgery Made Easy* by Steve Krug
- User Interface Engineering library and training events
- Nielsen Norman Group articles and training events
- Content Design courses run by Content Science Academy

Produce Less Content at Higher Production Quality— with Some Exceptions

Content polish might seem like a no-brainer, but it can be complicated. Content with more polish takes more time and resources to produce. Usually, I lean toward creating less content at a higher quality. Instead of cranking out mediocre company blog posts twice a week, for example, create an online magazine with a less frequent publishing cadence. Outdoor outfitter REI, for example, has elevated its content production to the point of creating award-nominated documentaries (**Figure 6.4**).

Figure 6.4: REI produces award-nominated documentaries.

A few important exceptions to this rule exist. Sometimes, quick and accurate content trumps polished content.

- **Social media and engagement.** In the context of social media, people have a higher tolerance for lower production quality. Grandparents, for example, are delighted to see pictures of their children playing soccer while the game is happening, even if the pictures are not perfect. In a similar way, your customers might find pictures from your company event more compelling if you share them while the event is happening instead of waiting to select and touch up the shots.

- **Emergencies or crises.** Timely, accurate content on your website, social media, and other touchpoints is much more important than polish.

USEFULNESS AND RELEVANCE/MEANING

Offer content that your customers find useful and meaningful to their goals.

WHY IT MATTERS

In mining our ContentWRX data, we found that relevant content makes or breaks goal completion (**Figure 6.5**). If your content is relevant to your customers, they will be much more likely to make decisions or complete tasks.

PERCENTAGE OF GOAL COMPLETION BASED ON RATING OF CONTENT

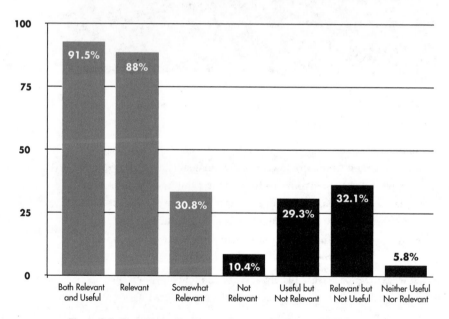

Figure 6.5: The effect of content rating on completing a goal

Additionally, if your customers view your content as both useful and relevant, they will be much more likely to view it as effective. The analysis of our ContentWRX data found that overall effectiveness scores (or what we call ContentWRX scores) were highest when people perceived content as both useful and relevant (**Figure 6.6**).

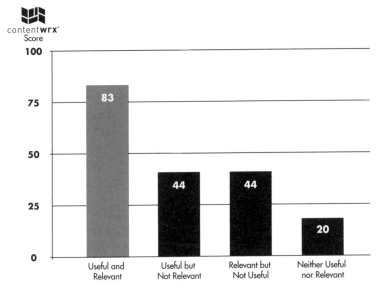

CONTENTWRX SCORES CORRELATE TO USEFULNESS AND RELEVANCE

Figure 6.6: The effect of content usefulness and relevance on content scores

So how do you make content useful and relevant, both in reality and in the hearts and minds of your customers? Let's review a few key tips.

TOP TIPS

These tips help address the reality of your content's usefulness and relevance/meaning.

Align Content Creation with Customer Personas and Journeys

The customer personas and journeys we discussed in Chapter 4 will be your go-to tools as you or your team create content. Review that information and ask yourself or your team

- Which customer persona or segment is this content for?
- At what stage or step in their journeys will customers use this content?
- How can this content answer the questions customers have?
- How can this content show sensitivity to customer emotions?

- How can this content help a customer make a decision or complete a task?
- How can this content help a customer get to the next stage or step in the journey?

Specify the Content Audience in the Content Itself

Your customers are busy, so don't make them waste time guessing who the content is for. Tell them. For example, *Harvard Business Review* proudly states it's the world's most influential management magazine. TD Ameritrade's *thinkMoney* says it's for "active traders." American Express Open Forum is not shy about saying it's for small businesses, especially small business owners. This practice not only will help clarify when content is relevant but also make it easier for customers to find.

This practice applies to a wide range of content, not just digital magazines. Sales content might require a version for business decision-makers and a version for technical experts, stakeholders, or decision-makers. Customer service and support content might require different versions for different roles or levels of expertise. In all those cases, stating who the intended audience is will help your customers know whether the content is pertinent.

State the Usefulness or Relevance in the Content Itself

Similar to specifying the content audience, don't make customers guess why the content is useful or relevant. Say it proudly. One technique I find helpful is to imagine your customers asking you, "So what?" Provide the answer immediately in the content. REI uses this technique in its advice and guidance content. The beginning of an article titled "Bike Suspension Basics" says

> Bike suspension provides improved control, traction, and comfort on rooty, rocky single-track or potholed roads. It is one of many factors that contribute to your riding enjoyment.

> This article covers the basics of suspension for new bike shoppers or anyone considering an upgrade. We then go on to provide a more detailed look at how suspension works.

And, it doesn't hurt to remind customers of the usefulness or relevance if the content is lengthy or requires deep interaction.

Check Whether You're Meeting the Needs of Advanced, Expert, or Specific Customers

If people report that content is not useful or relevant in ContentWRX, we ask why. The most common reason? Content is too general or basic (**Figure 6.7**). The least common reason? Content is too detailed or advanced.

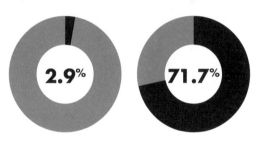

LACK OF DETAIL AND SOPHISTICATION LEADS TO LOW USEFULNESS AND RELEVANCE

Figure 6.7: The effect of content that is too general

24.7% of people who said that content was not useful indicated the content was too basic, general, or vague

2.9% of people who said that content was not useful indicated the content was too detailed or advanced

71.7% of people who said that content was not relevant indicated the content was too general

Consider whether you are repeating the same basic, high-level information again and again or tailoring content to the needs of important or high-value customers. For example, we worked with a credit monitoring company to develop a content strategy for consumers in a post-Equifax data breach world. We discovered that the credit monitoring content ecosystem repeats many basics over and over. We identified many exciting opportunities to better meet the needs of a wide range of consumers with different credit experiences. If you try to reach everyone with the basics, you risk reaching no one very effectively.

As another example, TD Ameritrade offers its customers a magazine called *thinkMoney*. This magazine does not regurgitate personal finance 101. Instead, this magazine offers material relevant to investors who are active traders. TD Ameritrade crunched the numbers and found that customers who engage with the magazine are significantly more likely to make a trade[2]—a return that the online broker finds worth the investment in sophisticated content.

The content effectiveness dimensions of findability, accuracy, polish, usefulness, relevance, and meaning are essential to earning the opportunity to influence your customers. Now, let's explore principles and techniques that will allow you to make the most of that opportunity.

REFERENCES

1. "Forecasting What Mobile Users Want: A 'Sunny Day' Strategy for Any Type of Weather," *Content Science Review* https://review.content-science.com/2017/08/forecasting-what-mobile-users-want-a-sunny-day-strategy-for-any-type-of-weather/

2. *Killing Marketing*, by Joe Pulizzi and Robert Rose

7 MAKE YOUR CONTENT INFLUENTIAL

· ·

Is your content compelling for your customers?

INFLUENCE IS THE NEW POWER—IF YOU HAVE INFLUENCE, YOU CAN CREATE A BRAND.
—Michelle Phan, YouTube personality

THE FORCE WILL BE WITH YOU. ALWAYS.
—Obi-Wan Kenobi

When you make your content effective, you earn the opportunity to influence your customers. Your content becomes like the Force in *Star Wars*. If you master it wisely, you can have a powerful positive impact. How can you make the most of that opportunity? Principles from rhetoric and psychology can help. Let's walk through these principles and techniques to apply them to your content.

RHETORIC: THE STUDY OF INFLUENCE

Despite its practical value, rhetoric is a lost art. We don't learn it in school, especially in the United States. (I didn't come across the topic much until graduate school.) Even worse, rhetoric is sometimes mistaken for a dark art. Politicians abuse it by making empty promises or hijacking our attention. Let's move forward by looking back at what the ancient Greeks (and other smart rhetoricians) actually had in mind.

The philosopher Aristotle defined rhetoric as figuring out the best way to persuade in a situation. Today, Andrea Lunsford, a respected professor at Stanford University, defines rhetoric as "the art, practice, and study of human communication."[1] Over thousands of years, smart scholars and practitioners have debated the theory and scope of rhetoric. I've distilled many of the useful ideas from that debate into two principles for content.

NOTE: For even more principles, check out Appendix A.

THE TRIED-AND-TRUE THREE APPEALS

What's the number-one principle of rhetoric? Aristotle would say it's not one but three: the persuasive appeals. He introduced them in *Rhetoric* as ethos (credibility), logos (logic), and pathos (emotion).[2] This trio has shaped notions of persuasion ever since.

Aristotle insisted on always combining these appeals. First, let's turn to credibility.

Credibility: Why Customers Should Listen to You

Speak when the wise Yoda does, listen people do. (See what I did there?) Yoda has not only a distinct style but also credibility. This appeal focuses on why people should trust and listen to you or your organization. Typical points of credibility include

- **Experience:** You have a lot of it, or your experience is specialized.
- **Success:** You've achieved something important or are having success now.
- **Reputation:** People in the community know you as having a certain characteristic, expertise, or offering.
- **Endorsement/association:** A credible brand or person says you are credible or connects with you in a credible way.
- **Certification:** You have earned a certain security or achievement level.
- **Longevity:** You've been around for a while.
- **Similarity:** You have a lot in common with the users.

The less people know about you, the more you need to prove your credibility. In turn, when you're established, sometimes you need to prove that your credibility is still relevant. The trick is to convey your credibility without making people yawn or think you're boasting. So let's look at how content can show your credibility in today's digital world.

Quality Content Over Time + Signature Content Types

You'll build a reputation as a trusted resource if you publish consistently good content over time. It's like being the person who reliably says something useful. What's even better? Becoming known for a particular approach to content.

- **Reviews, awards, and other recognition:** Focus on useful praise from sources your customers know and value.
- **Quotes:** Pick quotes from people your users respect and can relate to. If you're not a media property, business partnerships or alliances serve a similar purpose.
- **Expert contributions:** If a respected expert contributes content to your website, you gain credibility. In turn, if you're invited to be the expert contributor, you gain credibility. American Express Open Forum, a knowledge center for small businesses, offers content from their own experts as well as from outside thought leaders.

- **Curated content from credible sources:** Curating content is showcasing good content in a unique way. When you curate content from credible sources, you enhance your own credibility.

- **References:** When you ground your facts with references, you not only ensure you're telling the truth but also align with credible sources.

- **Brand, organization, or product history:** Sometimes, your organization or product has a rich and relevant history. The original Mini Cooper, for example, was designed to offer less expensive and more efficient transportation in the 1960s. Mini Cooper's website makes that story pertinent to today's environmental concerns.

- **Security and privacy cues:** When you ask people to share personal information, you need to show that your website is safe by displaying lock icons, security certifications, or similar cues. Provide easy access to your privacy policy or terms and put them in plain language.

- Now let's turn to the second appeal, logic.

Logic: Your Argument

It's whether your reasoning is formed well (also known as being valid). If logic were a *Star Wars* character, it would be the matter-of-fact C3P0. At a minimum, good reasoning comprises these key elements:

- **Claim:** What you assert to be true, such as a value proposition.

- **Evidence:** What supports your claim, such as facts, statistics, and testimonials.

- **Warrant:** Why you can make the claim based on the evidence, or your "leap in logic." Sometimes, the warrant is implied because it is an assumption (or a set of assumptions).

Your argument generally is good if

- Your claim is likely true when your evidence is true.

- Customers can understand the warrant quickly.

As a simple example, REI claims it is the first US-based travel company to become 100 percent carbon neutral. The evidence is that REI buys credits to support renewable energy (such as solar and wind). The warrant is that the renewable energy work neutralizes carbon emissions, so buying those credits compensates for REI's emissions.

Even if you form solid logic, your customers make or break it. Users must accept your evidence as good evidence. For example, REI emphasizes that it buys energy credits from the respected Bonneville Environmental Foundation. Your customers must also have enough in common with you to understand the assumptions. In the case of REI, their customers tend to care about the environment, and people who care about the environment are likely familiar with carbon credits.

Often, the more you ask of people's time or money, the more evidence you'll need to offer. Many people spend more time researching to buy a car than they do to buy driving gloves, for instance. That's why AutoTrader.com offers not only car advertisements but also a wealth of content with which to research features, performance, expert opinion, and more.

While most web content involves at least some reasoning, certain content types lend themselves more to articulating an argument:

- Blog posts
- Media articles or editorials
- Expert reviews
- Product or service descriptions
- White papers, fact sheets, or reports
- Interviews

In addition, certain content types make good evidence to support an argument:

- Charts, graphs, and data visualizations
- Testimonials, case studies, and similar stories

Avoid These Argument Mistakes

For airtight arguments, don't let these mistakes (also called fallacies) bubble up in your reasoning:

- **Generalizing hastily**, or drawing a conclusion based on an odd example (edge case) or a very small set of examples. Example: Search engine optimization (SEO) will double all companies' website traffic because SEO doubled one company's website traffic.

- **Distracting with a red herring**, or making an emotionally charged point that isn't relevant. Example: We should spend half of our interactive budget on SEO, unless we want our competitors to trample us like they did on that customer satisfaction survey.

- **Confusing cause with correlation**, or claiming that one event caused another only because the events happened at (or close to) the same time. Example: My company hired an SEO expert, and the next day my dog died. Hiring the SEO expert killed my dog.

  Of course, identifying correlations can be valuable, as we have found in our research of content effectiveness. It's helpful in planning your content approach to know that if customers have trouble finding your content, the content will not be as effective, even if we do not yet know the detailed, scientific cause for this correlation. The danger is in overstating correlation in a way that leads to faulty conclusions.

- **Sliding down the slippery slope**, or exaggerating that a situation will lead to a catastrophic chain of events. Example: If you don't spend lots of money on SEO, then you'll lose all of your prospective customers, and then your sales will plummet, and then the global economy will weaken, and then we will have political unrest that leads to nuclear war.

- **Jumping on the bandwagon**, or relying *only* on the evidence that other people are doing it. Example: Your competitors are spending lots of money on SEO. You should too.

The first two appeals address mostly our head. Now, let's address the heart with the appeal to emotion.

Emotion: Keeping Interest and Motivating Action

The emotional appeal is how you tap into people's emotions to hold their interest, gain their sympathies, or motivate them to act. If this appeal were a *Star Wars* character, it would be Jar Jar Binks. Kidding. It could be a number of characters, but Princess Leia stands out with her hologrammed, passionate plea to Obi-Wan Kenobi for help.

Appealing to emotion involves these related elements:

- **Tone:** The mood conveyed through your words, images, and other content.

- **Style:** Vivid word choice or imagery that's charged with emotion.

Let's look at a simple yet clever example from MailChimp. Instead of a typical name, MailChimp calls one of its email plans "Growing Business" (**Figure 7.1**). What entrepreneur doesn't aspire to grow?

Content offers many opportunities to charm your customers' emotions.

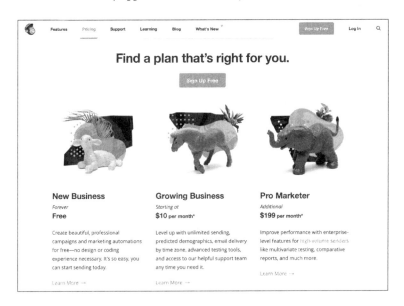

Figure 7.1: MailChimp taps into emotion with the plan name "Growing Business."

Voice

The personality or feel of your content. Two very different examples are Bliss and HowStuffWorks.com. Bliss is sassy, whereas HowStuffWorks is dissecting (**Figure 7.2**).

Figure 7.2: Bliss has a sassy voice, and HowStuffWorks has an analytical voice.

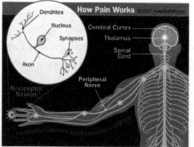

Sensory Detail

When you portray how things look, sound, smell, taste, or feel, you trigger people's gut reactions. Lindt, for instance, describes how wonderfully chocolate engages all five senses, tempting a chocoholic like me (**Figure 7.3**).

Figure 7.3: Lindt uses sensory detail to evoke emotion.

Associations with Words and Images

Beyond their literal meanings, words and images stir up feelings (also called connotations). MailChimp tapped into this positive association with the word *growing* in one of its email plan names.

Rhetorical Devices

Rhetorical devices are tools that enhance content emotionally. Following are some text examples, but you can apply many of these devices to images, video, or audio.

- **Hyperbole**, or over-the-top exaggeration, usually meant to be funny. Example: I love quality content so much that I want to marry it.

- **Irony**, or when the literal and intended meanings are out of sync; often intended to be funny. Example: You should publish the blog post that you paid someone $10 to write for you.

- **Simile**, or comparing unlike things. Example: This stagnant content is like a cesspool.

- **Rhetorical question**, or a question that creates a dramatic effect rather than asks for a literal answer. Example: Do we really want to keep creating terrible content?

- **Personification**, or adding personality or human qualities to a concept or object. Example: The website regurgitated content from 1999 at me.

The principle of the three appeals will take you far in making your content influential. But you can make your content even more influential with the principle of identification.

IRRESISTIBLE IDENTIFICATION

Identification is overcoming our differences to find common ground. It's the key principle for helping you attract the right people. Rhetorician Kenneth Burke defined identification as "any of the wide variety of means by which an author may establish a shared sense of values, attitudes, and interests with his [or her] readers [users]."[3] When users identify with you, they're more likely to be drawn to you.

Identify on the Right Level

We connect with people who are like us on superficial and deep levels. We can identify quickly with people who appear to be just like us. People connect more intensely to people in a similar role or with like values, interests, and beliefs. Not everyone will identify with you or your company's brand, and that's okay.

To attract the right people, content can help in many ways.

Persona/Character/Spokesperson

It's representing your organization with a person or character (or two or three) who relates well to your users. For example, HowStuffWorks offers a collection of podcasts hosted by relevant personalities. The most popular is *Stuff You Should Know*. On this podcast, self-proclaimed geeks Josh and Chuck banter about, well, stuff they think other geeks should know (**Figure 7.4**).

Figure 7.4: Josh and Chuck represent geekdom for HowStuffWorks.

User-Generated Content

Your users can represent you well. How? Through comments and content they contribute to your social networking space. The right potential customers will identify with your current customers. The trick is to facilitate the discussion so that it stays true to your brand and your users.

Cause Content

Another approach is to create content around a cause. Research from the public relations firm Edelman has found that supporting a cause could even inspire users to switch brands.[4] Select a cause that fits your brand values and your users' values. For example, REI devotes much content to environmental concerns (**Figure 7.5**).

Figure 7.5: The environment is a cause close to the hearts of many REI users and relates to REI's brand as an outdoor outfitter.

In the United States, REI even turned the day after Thanksgiving, Black Friday, into a cause with the #optoutside campaign. Black Friday is now as much about being thankful for the outdoors as it is about shopping.

Story Content

Still another approach to identification is telling a story, or narrative. A story allows you to bring values to life in a memorable, even entertaining, way.[5] Because a story often involves credibility, logic, and emotion, it makes a strong, influential impact. You can find a story in almost anything, but I find two types work well for practical purposes.

- **Brand/organization story:** If you're a startup, tell the tale of solving a tough problem or making a big change to help people. Grasshopper, for example, offers the concise but compelling story of its founding (**Figure 7.6**). If you're more established, explore your history or the story of an innovation or accomplishment.

Figure 7.6: Grasshopper tells the tale of its entrepreneurial roots.

- **Client/customer case study:** Case studies recount how you help your users. One approach is dramatization.

- A different approach is to present actual customer stories. A series of iPhone videos, for instance, showcase real users explaining how the iPhone saved the day. In one, a pilot recalls how he looked up the weather on the iPhone to help his flight avoid a three-hour delay (**Figure 7.7**).

Figure 7.7: A pilot explains how the iPhone helped him.

Although Burke defined identification in the 1950s, I wonder whether he had a crystal ball that let him glimpse the 21st century. He felt that identification could happen within a short paragraph, in a long series of communications over time, and in everything in between. Every bit of content is an opportunity to strengthen identification. Now let's turn to some principles from psychology.

PSYCHOLOGY: THE SCIENCE OF INFLUENCE

Scientific research tells us a lot about how we're influenced. But we don't learn about it in Psychology 101. The field's piles of research, however, offer a wealth of insight into what influences our minds. For this chapter, I've selected two principles to feature.

> NOTE: For more principles, check out Appendix A.

If I had to name a theme for these principles, I'd say it's *shortcuts*. People don't have the time and energy to research and think exhaustively about every little decision, even if they'd like to do so. Often without realizing it, people rely on these principles as timesavers.

FRAMING: GUIDING ATTENTION

A frame is a set of expectations, values, and assumptions that acts like a filtering lens. It leads us to see certain details and not others. As a simple example, let's say we're working with a project manager and a creative director. We have certain expectations for each role. If the project manager didn't create a project timeline, we'd notice and probably complain. If a creative director didn't create a project timeline, however, we probably wouldn't notice.

Framing is packaging an idea, issue, or choice in terms of the frame. Framing can lead people to understand a concept quickly and even favorably. For example, if we describe an idea to a project manager, we might stress that it saves time, avoids rework, and increases efficiency. In fact, that's exactly how 37signals talks about its project management software, Basecamp (**Figure 7.8**).

People will respond to the same choice differently when it is framed in different terms. Research suggests that a negative frame, especially describing a "loss," prompts a powerful emotional reaction in people.[6] It's so strong that people will even make a risky choice to avoid feeling the loss. The book *How We Decide*, by Jonah Lehrer, describes it this way:

> This human foible is known as the framing effect… the effect helps explain why people are much more likely to buy meat when it's labeled 85 percent lean instead of 15 percent fat. And why twice as many patients opt for surgery when told there's an 80 percent chance of their surviving instead of a 20 percent chance of their dying."[7]

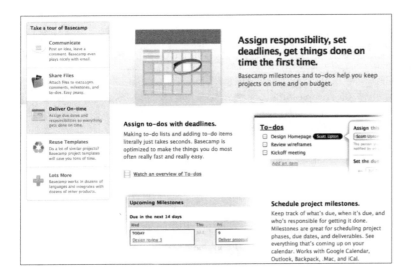

Figure 7.8: Basecamp taps into a project manager's frame of reference.

Negative frames aren't always bad. They simply spark a lot of emotional brain activity, so they're like playing with fire. Consider these statements:

- If you improve your SEO, you will gain 5000 new customers each year.

- If you do not improve your SEO, your company will lose 5000 new customers each year.

From a framing perspective, the second statement is more explosive. So be extra careful with negative frames. Save them for points that deserve urgent attention and a strong response.

Related to framing, priming is another subtle way to get people's attention. It means introducing words, images, or ideas now to influence people's choices a little later. For example, asking people the day before an election whether they intend to vote can increase the chance they'll vote by up to 25 percent.[8] The reason priming works is that we tend to act on what we remember easily.

To kick priming up a notch, you can address how to act on the choice. In the voting example, if you also showed people a map pointing out where they should go to vote, you'd further boost the chance they'll vote. As Richard H. Thaler says in *Nudge*, "Often we can do more to facilitate good behavior by removing some small obstacle than by trying to shove people in a certain direction."[9]

From #metoo to Fake News: Altering the Agenda

In media, politics, and public relations, one aspect of framing is agenda setting, or influencing what stories the media covers and, consequently, what people think about. The *New York Times*, CNN, and other mass media outlets cover certain stories but not others, for example.

And within a story, mass media includes certain details and not others. The theory goes that people are more likely to think or chat about the stories and details that mass media covers. Whether you view agenda setting as a conspiracy or as gatekeeping, it happens because it's impossible to talk about all things at all times with all the details.

Or is it possible?

In the first edition of this book, I noted that websites, blogs, and social networking—together known as new media— were changing the agenda because they provide details that mass media does not and that they even influence mass media. And I noted that we did not yet know to what extent. Well, we now know more.

On one hand, we have movements such as #timesup and #metoo, where survivors of sexual harassment and abuse in entertainment, technology, sports, and other workplaces have told their stories. Mass media outlets such as the *New Yorker*, the *New York Times*, and the *Hollywood Reporter* have published highly credible stories about Harvey Weinstein, Louis C.K., Russell Simmons, Bryan Singer, Kevin Spacey, and several other powerful men. Many more stories and excruciating details about those men—and others, such as Matt Lauer, James Franco, and the disgraced abusive doctor for USA Gymnastics, Larry Nassar— have been revealed on Twitter, Facebook, and blogs. As the stories and details accumulated—and still do even as I write this—the pressure for action increased, resulting in resignations, canceled projects, prosecutions, and more. These movements represent the potential for mass media and new media to work together in engineering positive change. Issues such as workplace culture, women's equality, and more are now part of the agenda.

On the other hand, we have seen new media be manipulated to undercut credible, fact checked stories in mass media and to induce people to believe fabricated and potentially harmful stories ranging from the world is flat to immunizations cause autism. One of the most comprehensive and disturbing example of this manipulation surrounds the 2016 US presidential election. Donald Trump often quips about "mainstream" media being "fake news," but it turns out that fake news helped him win the election. As I write this, more and more details about the extent of this fake news manipulation, or disinformation campaign, are coming to light. While we are still learning how and why this abuse happened, one thing is clear: new media can have a powerful effect on setting the agenda.

Although I see downsides to new media, I don't think the solution is to bring the same level of gatekeeping as mass media often requires. That would impede the benefits of new media—getting details out quickly in a social context. Instead, we need commonsense governance. Running ads that look like news stories, for example, is unacceptable. So is using people's data without permission to craft disinformation campaigns. I'm only scratching the surface, and my hope is that by the time we hit the third edition of this book, we will have addressed the exploitable gaps in new media, so we gain the benefits and minimize the dangers.

Let's look at some specific ways to apply framing to content.

Theme/Key Messages

When Centers for Disease Control and Prevention (CDC) decided to redesign its Travelers' Health website (mentioned in Chapter 4), I advised on an approach to the content. CDC wanted to convey the risk that travelers face so that they take the right precautions—but not to the point that people fear traveling. One recommendation I made was to frame the travel precautions as smart planning to ensure that business remains productive and that vacations stay fun. You can see a rough concept of this approach in **Figure 7.9.**

Figure 7.9: Positive key messages convey that travel precautions are important but not scary.

Curation

For years, Starbucks has curated music that reflects its brand and cultural perspective. Starbucks created its unique frame of the musical world, and the frame resonated with customers. Starbucks even released its own successful CDs and sponsored a satellite radio channel. Now that Starbucks offers free wireless internet access to customers, the coffee brand has released its own digital network. On it, Starbucks curates exclusive content from the *New York Times*, Apple, and other select publishers.[10] This network is Starbuck's frame of the digital world.

OPEN Forum by American Express uses curation to frame the digital world for small businesses. Specifically, the Idea Hub features content from select business owners and industry experts about pertinent topics (**Figure 7.10**).

Figure 7.10: American Express curates quality content for small businesses.

CURATED EXPERTS PROVIDE CONTENT

Claim and Evidence

The way you state a claim and the evidence you choose to support the claim is an opportunity to use framing. For example, the website for the personal genomics and biotechnology company 23andMe frames sharing your DNA results with researchers as an opportunity to be a part of something bigger.

The company supports this claim with a range of compelling evidence that illustrates just how big in scope, meaning, and impact. This positive framing of the claim and evidence has convinced thousands of people to opt into sharing their DNA information with the 23andMe research network.

Reminder and Instruction

Is your body mass index healthy? Is it time for your kids' shots? When did you last visit the dentist? What does your insurance cover? Your family's health information adds up to a lot of content to manage. Electronic health records (EHRs) have potential to get it under control. Imagine Mint.com for your health.

One benefit of EHRs is that they remind us to keep up with healthy behaviors, such as keeping our checkup appointments. Although no longer available, I will always like the way Mayo Clinic Health Manager highlighted upcoming medical visits on its dashboard. What would make this reminder even better is an option to receive it via email or text (**Figure 7.11**).

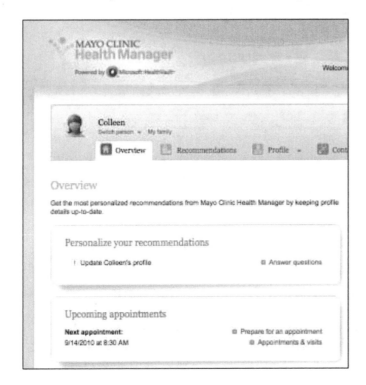

Figure 7.11: An EHR reminds me of an upcoming medical appointment.

And the Mayo Clinic Health Manager offered a wizard to guide you through preparing for a medical appointment. One of its features is that it compiles relevant sections of your personal health content so that you can bring it or send it to the doctor (**Figure 7.12**).

Figure 7.12: An EHR helps me get ready for the medical appointment.

And of course, other great examples of reminders and instruction have emerged in health and financial services. The Fitbit mobile application provides excellent examples of status updates, reminders, and instructions. The Capital One mobile application offers succinct and pertinent instructions and reminders for managing a credit card and more.

Reminder and instruction matter beyond electronic health records too. In the Travelers' Health project I mentioned, we paid close attention to instruction. Research had shown that travelers were confused about where to get travel immunizations. The best place to get them is a travel health clinic, not a personal physician. My content recommendations stressed going to the travel health clinic and suggested ways to make finding travel clinics easier. This approach tested well with users[11] (**Figure 7.13**).

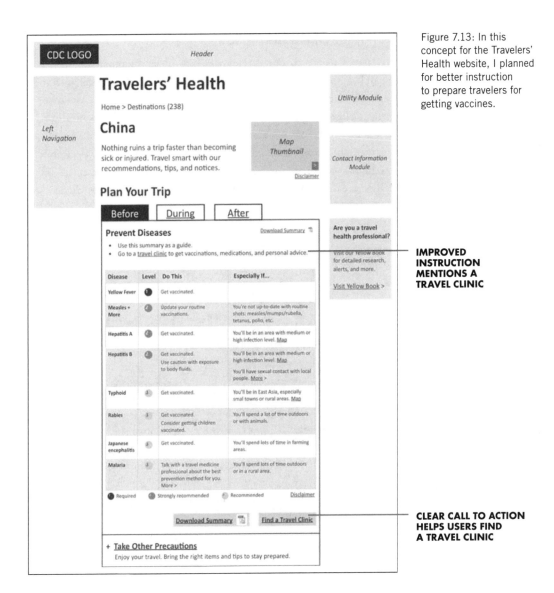

Figure 7.13: In this concept for the Travelers' Health website, I planned for better instruction to prepare travelers for getting vaccines.

Clearly, framing is a powerful and versatile principle for making your content influential. I'd like to share one more principle to consider for your content.

METAPHOR: A TIE THAT BINDS

Metaphor isn't just that pretty language that makes a comparison, such as "Shall I compare thee to a summer's day?"[12] It's more, as psychologists and linguists have learned. Cognitive scientist Steven Pinker says, "Metaphor really is a key to explaining thought and language."[13] More specifically, consumer psychology experts Gerald Zaltman and Lindsay Zaltman say that metaphors are "basic categories of patterned thinking and decision making."[14] Metaphors are the way we think and talk about our world. The Zaltmans even think that metaphors resonate more deeply than archetypes, a staple of marketing strategy (see the following sidebar).

Research-Proven Metaphors

The innovative research team of Gerald Zaltman and Lindsay Zaltman have found these metaphors to be the most common and compelling around the world. They've made the basic list freely available. (The examples noted below are simply my opinion.) For their take on discovering and using metaphors, read *Marketing Metaphoria*.

- **Balance** includes the ideas of equilibrium; adjusting, maintaining, or offsetting forces; and things as they should be. Example: Make It Right (makeitrightnola.org).

- **Transformation** involves changing states or status. Example: Mint.com.

- **Journey** addresses how the past, present, and future meet. Example: *Your Life, Your Money* (pbs.org/your-life-your-money/).

- **Container** involves keeping things in and keeping things out. Example: Shoeboxed.com.

- **Connection** encompasses feelings of belonging or exclusion. Example: American Express OPEN Forum (Connectodex).

- **Resource** involves acquisitions and their consequences. Example: TED.com ("Ideas worth spreading").

- **Control** covers mastery, vulnerability, and well-being. Example: 23andMe.

Tactically, metaphor often connects new or abstract ideas to something people already know. This connection helps people understand the ideas faster. That's especially helpful for technology, which changes quickly. Interaction design expert Dan Saffer has even said, "Everything one says about the computer is metaphor."[15] For example, when internet use spread in the late 1990s, the term "web page" described a website screen in terms of something familiar—a paper page. It's not really a page, though, so academics wanted to call a website screen a "node." Which term caught on?

Use Metaphors Sparingly

Psychologists and English professors agree that less is more. If you use too many metaphors, you risk confusing people. Focus more on selecting the right metaphor and reinforcing it in different ways. For example, the name Make It Right for a foundation suggests restoring or returning to balance. The website's references to rebuilding and renewal subtly support the metaphor (**Figure 7.14**).

Figure 7.14: The Make It Right Foundation uses metaphor subtly but effectively.

Build on Metaphors People Already Use

Metaphors are vital to how we think and talk, and your users use them to describe their needs and your industry. As you research and communicate with your current users—or with the users you want to attract—take note of the words and phrases they use. When it comes to the complexities of finance, for example, people might feel "stuck" or eager to "turn over a new leaf" or ready for a "fresh start." The personal finance service Mint.com taps into that metaphorical language brilliantly with its name alone, which suggests

- Herbal leaf known for its fresh smell and taste
- Source of new money

The name also happens to be short for the original name, Money Intelligence. (We should all be so lucky with our abbreviations.)

Apply Metaphor to Content

We can use the mighty metaphor almost anywhere in our web content to make us memorable and likable. Here are a few examples.

Name, Message, Call to Action

As the name implies, Designzillas humorously compares its web design agency to the Japanese monster (and sometimes hero) Godzilla. The agency sticks to this single metaphor throughout the concise site with copy and graphics (**Figure 7.15**).

Figure 7.15: Designzillas draws on one metaphor consistently.

This metaphor will make you laugh with messages and calls to action such as

- Is your website stuck in the stone age?
- We keep our clients on top of the food chain.
- Our agency has evolved into fire-breathing web designers.
- We are black belts in web-kwon-do.
- Call us today! We don't bite.

While funny and creative, this metaphor also positions Designzillas as a supernatural hero ready to rescue a client in need. That positioning taps into a deeper metaphor of transformation (see the sidebar "Research-Proven Metaphors").

Organization Story

Heroic metaphor is also prominent in the story of Adam and Eric, the founders of Method home care products. The story compares the founders to accidental superheroes (**Figure 7.16**).

our story

the proud brainparents of method and the very first people against dirty®.

Meet Adam Lowry and Eric Ryan, proud brainparents of method and the very first people against dirty®. Despite founding one of the fastest-growing private companies in America, and single-handedly turning the consumer-packaged-goods industry on its head, these two former roommates are quick to tell you that they're no heroes. And that's true. They're SUPER-heroes.* And like every great superhero, they gained their powers after being exposed to toxic ingredients. Cleaning supplies, to be precise. But rather than turning them green or granting them the ability to talk to fish, Eric and Adam's toxic exposure gave them something even better. An idea.

Eric knew people wanted cleaning products they didn't have to hide under their sinks. And Adam knew how to make them without any dirty ingredients. Their powers combined, they set out to save the world and create an entire line of home care products that were more powerful than a bottle of sodium hypochlorite. Gentler than a thousand puppy licks. Able to detox tall homes in a single afternoon.

Figure 7.16: Metaphor equates Adam and Eric to superheroes.

The founders are quick to tell you that they're no heroes. And that's true. They're SUPERheroes. And like every great superhero, they gained their powers after being exposed to toxic ingredients. Cleaning supplies, to be precise. But rather than turning them green or granting them the ability to talk to fish, Eric's and Adam's toxic exposure gave them something even better. An idea.

"Eric knew people wanted cleaning products they didn't have to hide under their sinks. And Adam knew how to make them without any dirty ingredients. Their powers combined, they set out to save the world and create an entire line of home care products that were more powerful than a bottle of sodium hypochlorite. Gentler than a thousand puppy licks. Able to detox tall homes in a single afternoon."

By now, you might have a lot of ideas for creating and curating effective, influential content. You're ready to make your content a force for good. Now is the perfect time to figure out how you will assess whether your content is working. That means it's time to plan content intelligence.

REFERENCES

1 Andrea Lunsford, stanford.edu/dept/english/courses/sites/lunsford/pages/defs.htm

2 Aristotle, *Rhetoric*

3 Kenneth Burke, *A Rhetoric of Motives* (University of California Press, 1969)

4 "The 2017 Earned Brand Study," edelman.com/earned-brand

5 Colleen Jones, "Become an Interactive Storyteller" imediaconnection.com/content/18041.imc

6 Jonah Lehrer, *How We Decide* (Houghton Mifflin Harcourt, 2009)

7 Jonah Lehrer, *How We Decide* (Hougton Mifflin Harcourt, 2009)

8 Richard H. Thaler, *Nudge* (Yale University Press, 2008)

9 Richard H. Thaler, *Nudge* (Yale University Press, 2008)

10 Jennifer Van Grove, "How Starbucks Plans to Capitalize on Free Wi-Fi" http://mashable.com/2010/08/12/starbucks-digital-network/

11 Colleen Jones, Kevin O'Connor, "Testing Content" IA Summit

12 Shakespeare, Sonnet 18

13 Steven Pinker, *The Stuff of Thought* (Viking, 2007)

14 Gerald Zaltman, Lindsay Zaltman, *Marketing Metaphoria* (Harvard Business School Press, 2008)

15 Dan Saffer, "The Role of Metaphor in Interaction Design" slideshare.net/dansaffer/the-role-of-metaphor-in-interaction-design

PRUDENCE: DEVELOP CONTENT INTELLIGENCE

Learn from your content and customers.

8 SET UP A CONTENT INTELLIGENCE SYSTEM

• •

Turn content data into actionable insight.

WHAT GETS MEASURED GETS MANAGED.

—Peter Drucker

REMEMBER: YOUR FOCUS DETERMINES YOUR REALITY.

—Qui-Gon Jinn, *Star Wars: The Phantom Menace*

Inspired by business intelligence, *content intelligence* is the term I use to refer to a system of collecting data related to your content and turning it into insight for content decisions and more. Let's walk through why your company needs content intelligence and the key elements of a content intelligence system.

WHY CONTENT INTELLIGENCE

Whether you're skeptical about needing content intelligence yourself or you need to convince someone else, rest assured that many reasons exist to embrace the data side of your content. Allow me to highlight five main reasons.

MAKE SMARTER CONTENT DECISIONS FOR BETTER BUSINESS RESULTS

With useful data about your content on tap, you can make higher-quality decisions about content and, ultimately, make the content more effective. Those content decisions might be strategic, such as investing in a new form of content, as REI did when it developed an original documentary series or as Netflix did when it created *House of Cards*. Or those content decisions might be tactical, such as when Netflix tested the performance of three versions of the art for a movie teaser. Both strategic and tactical content decisions benefit from data.

SHOW PROGRESS TO MOTIVATE CONTINUED CONTENT INNOVATION

We know from a variety of research that seeing progress motivates people. (For an excellent summary of this research and practical application, I highly recommend *The Progress Principle*, by Teresa Amabile.) It is difficult, if not impossible, to show content progress without clear data. I like how Ann Marie Gray, vice president of content at ASUG, explains the connection.[1]

> You should always be raising the bar for yourself. Nowadays, everything has become so data-driven, which allows us to see what's working, what content is driving results—but the value of that is what you do with it.

Similarly, Jung Suh of SAP describes the excitement of having data to inform content decisions.

> We are constantly creating and refining our content. With the right tools and processes, this is more exciting than daunting. We can see where our content is falling short, identify gaps, and zero in on emerging opportunities.[2]

MAKE FUTURE CONTENT ANALYSIS AND AUDITING EASIER AND INTEGRATED WITH GOVERNANCE

Often, companies wait until a redesign or until a replatforming or a digital transformation initiative becomes priority before they analyze their content in the way described in Chapter 4. Because content analysis has not happened in years, it's a big, expensive, slow job. When that analysis is finished, most companies return to "content as usual" and don't analyze again until they face another significant change. Wouldn't it make more sense to invest resources in ongoing content intelligence instead? That way, you can handle analysis for the next big change more efficiently, and you can make data part of your content governance.

While director of digital governance at Intel, Scott Rosenberg, nicely explained the role of data in governing content.

> As for addressing our content quantity issues, we focused on data. Content creation can certainly be a very personal and emotional topic. We realized that and decided to minimize as much as possible the emotional element by identifying clear, objective criteria to evaluate content against. We've learned from previous efforts at governing content that were too focused on just performance data only that we needed to take a multidimensional approach to evaluating content. Instead, in addition to performance data, we looked at strategic alignment to corporate priorities, content ROI, and resource commitments to support. This data-focused and collaborative approach resulted in far fewer escalations and emotional pleas from our stakeholders.[3]

GAIN INSIGHTS ABOUT YOUR CUSTOMERS

When customers interact with your content, they leave signals about who they are, what they need, what interests them, and more. Learning more about your customers not only helps with offering the right content for them but can also inform your marketing or sales approach, generate product and feature ideas, or innovate customer service. For example, CFA Institute—a not-for-profit association that credentials investment professionals—learned that prospective entrants into their credentialing program often compared attaining the Chartered Financial Analyst (CFA) credential with attaining an MBA. Consequently, the CFA Institute developed content to help prospects compare the options.

LAY THE FOUNDATION FOR ADVANCED CONTENT AUTOMATION

If you're thinking about scaling your approach to content, you might be thinking about content automation and how different types of artificial intelligence can help. I like the way you think. We'll talk more about content automation in Section V, but for now I will note that collecting data about your content helps. A lot.

I've covered five main reasons to embrace content intelligence, and you might think of others. Yet Content Science studies have found that even though most content professionals want content intelligence, only the most advanced companies are embracing it (**Figure 8.1**).

I once worked with an enterprise possessing one of the biggest data lakes in the world—a data lake rivaling that of Amazon—yet their content teams had no visibility into the data. The content teams operated in a data desert, making content decisions with no clue about their impact and no way to understand whether they were making progress toward goals. The content teams also lacked evidence about content impact to support their conversations with stakeholders. The content teams often felt powerless when stakeholders insisted on certain content solutions, terminology, or approaches and refused to collaborate. Instead of letting content teams thrive with the data lake, this company made their content teams parched for data-informed decisions, signals of progress, and productive collaboration.

The good news here is that you and your company face a tremendous opportunity to leapfrog most companies' sophistication with content and data by embracing content intelligence.

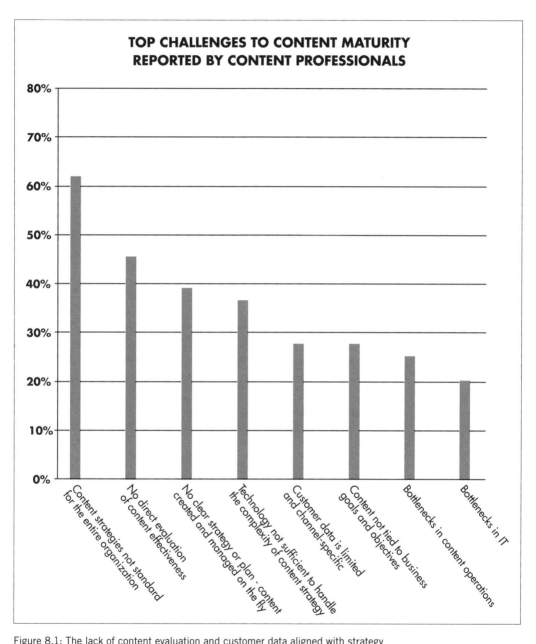

Figure 8.1: The lack of content evaluation and customer data aligned with strategy and goals signals a desire for content intelligence.

THE ELEMENTS OF A CONTENT INTELLIGENCE SYSTEM

The content intelligence approach consists of three main elements, as you can see in **Figure 8.2**.

A content intelligence system collects content-related data from multiple sources, and then analyzes that data to answer questions about content performance and more. Looking at the data through the lens of content is key. Let's explore each element of content intelligence, starting with getting the data.

GATHER CONTENT DATA FROM MULTIPLE SOURCES

Strive to collect two types of data: behavioral data and perception data.

Behavioral data tells you who your users are and what they do with your content, including how users find it and where they are engaging with it. For example, you might look at web analytics to understand actions that users are taking with your content that provide value to your organization. You may look at your channel analytics, such as phone calls or chat inquiries, to understand how content is supporting your sales and marketing efforts. And you might use business metrics, such as revenue or churn rate, to find large-scale correlations with your content efforts.

Perception data tells you what users think about the content and about your company or your offerings as a result of the content. You can review the substance of email, chat, and phone inquiries. You also can gain insight through polls, surveys, ratings, comments, reviews, and other ways of capturing the voice of the customer. And if your company has a strong social media presence, you can review the sentiment and comments about your content or topics covered by your content.

Of course, data by itself is not inherently valuable to any organization. Your data becomes valuable when you're determining what's happening with your content, which leads us to the second element of content intelligence.

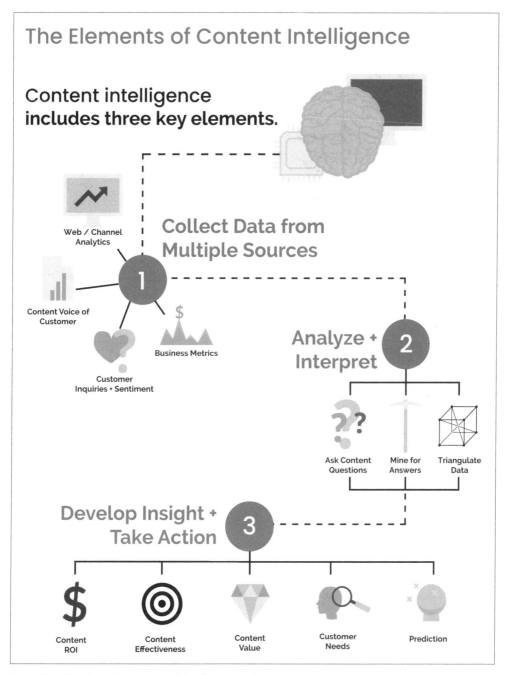

Figure 8.2: The elements of a content intelligence system

Tools That Can Help

Consider taking advantage of the following tools if your company already has them, or add them to your tool kit if not.

Sample web and content analytics tools:

- Adobe Analytics
- Google Analytics
- ContentWRX
- NewsCred
- Percolate
- Kapost
- Contently

Sample social and media analytics and sentiment tools:

- Hootsuite
- Mention
- Zoho Social
- Falcon.io
- Meltwater
- Cision

Sample voice of customer tools:

- ContentWRX
- Foresee
- Qualtrics
- Medallia

For more tools, see Appendix C.

ANALYZE AND INTERPRET THE DATA

Once you have begun gathering data, establish an approach to analysis and interpretation focused on your content by following three steps:

1. Ask content questions.
2. Mine the data for answers.
3. Triangulate the data.

Each of these three steps requires that you get the right people and processes in place to accomplish them.

Ask Content Questions

Asking the right questions about your content's performance requires you to define a goal for your content that aligns with your overall business objectives and that supports growth. What are you looking to achieve with this content? You can summarize this goal by completing the sentence, "This content will _____ ."

Diverse types of content have diverse goals. For example, product comparison tools, product pages, and demonstration videos guide customers along the buying journey. Your ultimate goal for this content is to make a sale.

Once you know your content's end goal, you define how your content can reach that goal. What are the elements of your content's performance that will add up to the accomplishment of that goal? These are evaluation dimensions and are what you can directly measure. Some examples of these dimensions are:

- **Reach**—the number of customers who use your content, and whether it's growing

- **Engagement**—how well your content commands your customers' attention

- **Perception**—how your content influences the way people feel about your company or offerings

- **Comprehension**—how well your content helps your customers understand a topic, issue, or problem

Once you've defined the dimensions across which your content needs to succeed, you're ready to start asking questions about its performance. Determining the right questions will help you understand what data you need to measure. For example, to understand how your content drives engagement, you might ask:

- Are our customers regularly returning to the content?

- Do our customers read and click our emails?

- Are our customers looking at multiple pieces of content on our site?

- Are our customers clicking or otherwise engaging with our interactive content?

You can organize your questions in a matrix, such as the sample matrix in **Table 8.1**.

Table 8.1 A Sample Content Intelligence Matrix

SALES CONTENT	
Goal: Increase sales scope and speed by providing useful, compelling content to support customers in their buying journey.	
Engagement	• Are our customers regularly returning to the content?
	• Do our customers read and click our emails?
	• Are our customers looking at multiple pieces of content on our site?
	• Are our customers clicking or otherwise engaging with our interactive content?
Perception	• Do customers understand and see the value of our products after viewing this content?
	• Does this content help customers view our brand more positively?
Conversion	• Are customers interested in learning more about our products after viewing this content?
	• Is this content contributing to sales?

After you determine the questions to ask, you can look to the data for answers.

Mine Data for Answers

This step requires you to use the data you've gathered to answer the questions you have about your evaluation dimensions. For example, you might approach your questions about your content's engagement with the following:

- Are our customers regularly returning to the content? Use Returning Users from your web analytics platform, as well as the Sessions/User metric.

- Do our customers read and click our emails? Use Opens, Clicks, and Click-to-Open Rate from your email marketing platform.

- Are our customers looking at multiple pieces of content on our site? Use Bounce Rate and Pages/Session to see how many users view multiple pieces of content and how many total pieces of content are viewed.

- Are our customers clicking or otherwise engaging with our interactive content? Create Events with your tag manager to track clicks, time on content, and other forms of engagement with interactive content in your web analytics platform.

You can even update your content intelligence matrix to include the data points that are likely to help you answer the questions.

Once you know exactly which data you need and where to find it, you can cut down your measurement data to the metrics that make the most sense for speaking to your content's impact. Then, you can review the data for relationships and more.

Triangulate the Data

When you have the data to answer your questions, you can review it further to search for relationships, causations, and influencing factors. For example, if you see spikes or dips in one metric, look for correlations in the activity of a different one.

While working with the American Cancer Society, there was a time when we noticed a sharp dip in engagement with their "Get Involved" content. Their time onsite and pages/visit metrics had decreased considerably, and when we looked at ContentWRX results we saw that perceptions of this content's findability and usefulness had also dipped.

When you notice a correlation, you can look into potential causes for the results. We looked further at the ContentWRX results and discovered that mobile users reported they were seeing error messages as they tried to sign up for American Cancer Society events. The Society was then able to fix the mobile content and experience.

Finally, explore how to report and visualize the data so you can better see your content's impact. Consider creating a standardized report or dashboard to make presenting and socializing content performance an easily repeatable task. (See **Figure 8.3** for a few examples that Content Science has helped create.)

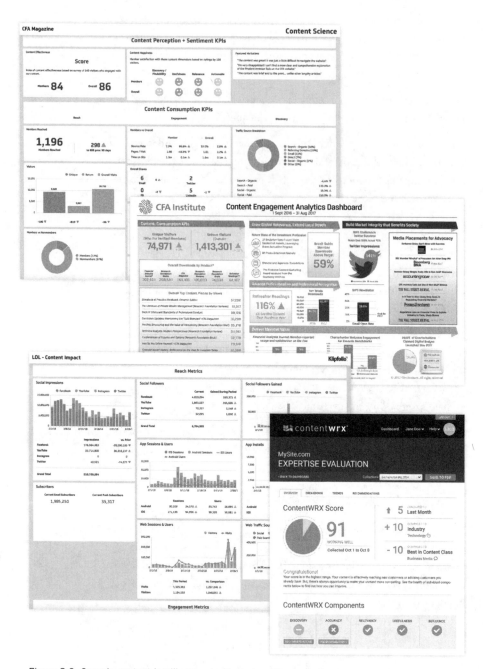

Figure 8.3: Sample content intelligence dashboards and reports

> **Tools That Can Help**
>
> A variety of dashboard and reporting tools can help businesses large and small bring together content data in useful ways.
>
> - Klipfolio
> - Google Data Studio
> - Qlik
> - Power BI

DEVELOP INSIGHT AND TAKE ACTION

Once you're collecting the right data and you have a system for analysis in place, developing insights that inform content decisions comes easily. You can better understand your content's effectiveness, estimate your return on content investment, and more. We'll talk more about how to gain insight and take action in Chapters 9 and 10.

REFERENCES

1   Content Science, "Content Operations and Leadership Study."

2   Brightedge, "Content Performance Marketing" whitepaper

3   "Intel Addresses Modern Marketing Challenges Through Digital Governance," *Content Science Review* https://review.content-science.com/2016/10/ intel-addresses-modern-marketing-challenges-through-digital-governance/

9 SECRETS TO USING CONTENT INTELLIGENCE

• •

Decide to become a content genius.

LIFE IS POKER, NOT CHESS.
—Annie Duke, *Thinking in Bets*

SIR, THE POSSIBILITY OF SUCCESSFULLY NAVIGATING AN ASTEROID FIELD IS APPROXIMATELY THREE THOUSAND SEVEN HUNDRED AND TWENTY TO ONE!
—C3PO

NEVER TELL ME THE ODDS.
—Han Solo

"Life comes down to decisions," my mom said to me one Sunday after-noon at least a decade ago. I appreciated the comment at the time because I had watched my mom and dad navigate many tough decisions together. For example, they took a chance on my dad starting a company the same year they started a family—when I was born. Even chancier, the company focused on the relatively new field of industrial automation—using electri-cal controls to perform tasks and streamline processes in factories. As you can imagine, my parents made many, many other decisions from there. The company ultimately succeeded. (Hopefully, they think the family did too.)

But I didn't fully appreciate my mom's comment about decisions until now. Since my mom's comment, the wealth of research about decisions that comes from economics, psychology, neuroscience, persuasion, manage-ment, sociology, and even law has become much more accessible. And I find it valuable for gaining insight and taking action in life as well as in content.

In this chapter, we'll take some inspiration from decision-making experts to help you develop quality insights and take effective action based on your content intelligence. This chapter also provides tips and examples to jump-start your approach to insight and action. After all, if you collect and analyze content data but don't *use* it to make content decisions, you might as well not have any data.

CONTENT IS POKER, NOT CHESS

In the excellent book *Thinking in Bets: Making Smarter Decisions When You Don't Have All the Facts*, poker genius and former psychology PhD candidate Annie Duke asserts that most decisions in life are much more like playing a hand of poker than like playing a game of chess. Why? The difference is the amount of data available to inform your decision. In chess, all the information is available. You see the move your opponent makes, and you know all the possible moves you can make in response. How-ever, in poker you know your cards. If you're really dedicated, you might know the odds of your pair of 3s winning. In the course of a hand, more information—such as the house's cards, your opponents' betting behavior, and even some of your opponents' cards—becomes revealed to you. But you never have *all* the information available to you. You are constantly deciding whether and how to bet with only partial data. Annie notes in the book that

> Poker is a game of incomplete information. It is a game of decision-making under conditions of uncertainty over time. (Not coincidentally, that is close to the definition of game theory.) Valuable information remains hidden. There is also an element of luck in any outcome. You could make the best possible decision at every point and still lose the hand, because you don't know what new cards will be dealt and revealed. Once the game is finished and you try to learn from the results, separating the quality of your decisions from the influence of luck is difficult.

> In chess, outcomes correlate more tightly with decision quality. In poker, it is much easier to get lucky and win or get unlucky and lose. If life were like chess, nearly every time you ran a red light you would get in an accident (or at least receive a ticket). But life is more like poker. You could make the smartest, most careful decision in firing a company president and still have it blow up in your face. You could run a red light and get through the intersection safely—or follow all the traffic rules and signals and end up in an accident.

I agree with Duke about life decisions, and I also find that tennis decisions and content decisions are like poker. (I think this explains why even though I love poker, I don't play often. My brain is spent from all those life, content, and tennis decisions!) Even with the most robust content analysis, you will never have all the information about your customers, context, or even your business (if it's large) available. If a content expert tells you they know the exact formula to achieve success with your content, run away. That "expert" is crazy, an amateur, or both. Your content decisions are like poker bets, not chess formulas.

CRITICAL CONTENT DECISIONS TO MAKE

Content involves myriad decisions as you source/create, distribute, and manage it. But just as key poker decisions come down to whether to bet and, if you do, how much, I find that content decisions come down to three types. Understanding these types of decisions will help you identify when such a decision is appropriate for your content situation.

STAY THE COURSE, BUT OPTIMIZE OR SCALE

You find that your approach to content is working pretty well. But you wonder whether it could work even better. These decisions relate to whether to make changes that optimize or scale content that is already pretty effective. For example, after succeeding with *House of Cards,* Netflix has tried to repeat that success. Netflix reviewed intelligence about which content has been effective with which audiences and developed new content ranging from *Daredevil* (one of my faves) to *The Crown* to the prequel to *Wet Hot American Summer.* Much of this original content has succeeded in terms of critical and popular acclaim. Only Netflix knows the detailed performance numbers for its original content across markets, but the public data about Netflix shows that they keep adding subscribers around the world at an explosive rate.[1]

In another example, the home security company Blink created a set of content promoted by email to onboard new customers. Blink conducted analysis, such as surveying customers about their top questions when they signed up, to make that content effective. But Blink didn't stop there; the team constantly tests different combinations of text and images for onboarding and more. Email manager Daniel Hinds notes, "I test things bracket style—the winner of one test goes up against something new the next time, and we see who lasts."[2]

When tackling this type of decision, consider questions such as

- What can we learn from the elements of this content that are working well?
- Which elements of the content could be even more effective? In what way?
- How could we repeat this success with these customers?
- How could we repeat this success in another area of the business?

FIX A PROBLEM

Your content's impact falls short of your expectations. Or your content has caused or exacerbated another problem. For instance, I've seen credit monitoring companies obtusely offer content laden with marketing-ese to consumers who come to them for help repairing their credit after suffering identity theft. That approach causes a host of problems, including lost sales, brand/company hatred that leads to brand adversaries (instead of advocates), and more regulatory oversight of their communications to consumers.

As another example, the American Cancer Society discovered a content problem when reviewing their data from Google Analytics and ContentWRX. The content problem centered on Road to Recovery, a unique program that connects cancer patients who need rides to cancer treatment with volunteers who can drive them. These two different audiences sought answers to their questions from one web page. The data indicated that the web page was leaving both audiences with more questions than answers—and lots of frustration. So the American Cancer Society successfully reorganized the content and offered pages with content tailored to each audience: the patients and the volunteers.[3]

When facing this type of decision, think about questions such as

- Were our expectations for this content reasonable? Did the content really fall short, or were our expectations unrealistic?
- What is the cause or source of the problem?
  - Is it the content itself? If so, what limits its effectiveness?
  - Is it the way the content is promoted, delivered, presented, or organized?
  - Is it a lack of alignment between the content and customer needs or tastes?
- To fix the problem, do we need to change the content or do we need to remove it or stop producing it altogether?
- What have we learned from this shortfall or problem?

INNOVATE OR ADDRESS A NEW OPPORTUNITY

You want to take your content to the next level or make the most of a new opportunity. Let's return to our Netflix example. Netflix has sought aggressive expansion beyond the United States into international markets, taking great care to translate and localize content for those markets. Netflix has painstakingly tried to make every bit of content, from subtitles to marketing descriptions, resonate with each international market. This hard work is paying off, resulting in 5.46 million of its 7.1 million new subscribers residing outside the US in the first quarter of 2018. With the success of its original content and its international expansion, Netflix has decided to bet $10 million on more content, including the marketing of that content, and only $1.3 billion on technology in 2018.[4]

As a different example, the marketing automation company MailChimp recognized an opportunity to gain more empathy for its customers, many of whom run online retail stores. Instead of imagining what being in their customers' shoes is like, MailChimp decided to sell shoes. That's right, MailChimp created its own online retail store and sold products for charity. This effort, aptly named Project What's in Store, allowed the MailChimp team to learn firsthand about the decisions many of its customers face, the tools they use, and much more. Project lead Melissa Metcalf calls this approach "Becoming the Customer." Not only did MailChimp gain empathy and raise money for charity, but the company also created a wealth of new content explaining lessons learned during the project *and* built a new email list topping 1 million subscribers. What's in Store now also showcases lessons that MailChimp customers share about succeeding in ecommerce. (Curious about this content? You can check it out at mailchimp.com.)

When facing this type of decision, consider questions such as

- How can we learn more about and meet the new interests, needs, and expectations expressed by our customers?
- How can we learn more about and meet the needs of new customers we did not expect?
- How do we need to adjust our content to meet the needs of customers in new markets?
- How could we package or deliver our content differently to make our products or services better?
- How could we monetize our content more effectively?

How can content intelligence help you tackle these types of decisions? I'd like to offer four useful ways.

WAYS TO INFORM CONTENT DECISIONS WITH CONTENT INTELLIGENCE

To get you started with using content intelligence, let's review four handy approaches that are based on the Insight + Action element from our diagram of content intelligence (**Figure 9.1**).

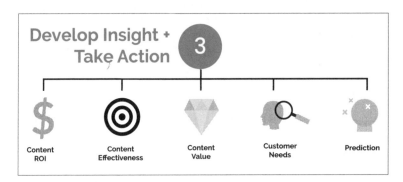

Figure 9.1: The third element of content intelligence, Insight + Action

ASSESS CONTENT EFFECTIVENESS

Understand what elements of your content are working well and what elements have an opportunity to be even more effective. This insight helps you identify elements you could optimize or elements that might be causing a problem. For instance, when the Centers for Disease Control and Prevention (CDC) realized travelers were calling them with questions about vaccinations that their web content should have answered, the agency investigated and identified problems with their content's findability, accuracy, and usefulness. The agency then worked on addressing those problems by changing the organization of the content, clarifying key points, removing less important content, and making the format easier to scan and use.

CALCULATE CONTENT ROI OR VALUE

Know whether the impact your content is making is worth the cost. CDC, for example, saved money on supporting travelers' calls after making their web content more effective. As another example, in 2017 the Weather Channel launched new features and content in their mobile applications.

The goal? To engage users in new ways. As mentioned earlier in this book, people turn to apps when the weather might be unfavorable or severe—not so much on sunny days. So content strategist Lindsay Howard worked with the team to think through sunny-day scenarios and develop ideas that would offer and promote relevant content. The results? Howard reports

> Immediately, our "sunny day" efforts started seeing results. Since launching, we increased performance in double digits across all priority metrics, including visits per user, sponsorship traffic, total impressions, and retention. This is particularly significant in an app world, where every percentage point counts. International engagement, a key factor in global relevance and expansion, skyrocketed. A priority metric for content strategy, click-through rate, went up 23 percent in less than three months.[5]

The results were so valuable that the Weather Channel has committed to exploring other ways that the strategic planning of content can help their business.

Table 9.1 summarizes a few common ways to consider content ROI or value.

Think your company has to be big to get a return on content investment? Think again. In the book *The Million-Dollar, One-Person Business*, Elaine Pofeldt notes that one common type of such business is information provider, such as a business that charges a small fee for access to a newsletter or other content. Other types of small and successful businesses, such as niche online retailers who use platforms such as Shopify and email tools such as MailChimp, have found content invaluable for everything from sales to customer support. Content helps automate many of these functions, allowing the business to avoid adding overhead when increasing revenue.

DEEPEN UNDERSTANDING OF CUSTOMERS

Learn more about who your customers are, what they need, and what they prefer from your content. For example, Kraft has used the insight they gained about their customers' interests—gleaned from those customers' interactions with their content—to make their advertising more effective.

Table 9.1 ROI

BUSINESS FUNCTION + CONTENT TYPE	POTENTIAL CONTENT ROI OR VALUE
Marketing	• Increase awareness of brand or product • Change perception of brand or product • Increase reach or engagement with right customers • Increase registrants or subscribers • Increase sales leads • Reduce cost per sales lead
Sales	• Increase sales or sales of certain products or services • Decrease cost per sale • Increase paid subscribers • Accelerate sales or paid subscriptions • Reduce returns • Increase upsell or cross-sell • Increase repeat sales
Customer Experience	• Increase use of or engagement with brand, product, or service • Increase referrals • Increase brand or product advocacy • Improve customer satisfaction • Increase upsell, upgrade, or cross-sell • Reduce churn • Reduce returns • Reduce support inquiries
Service and Support	• Reduce costs • Reduce churn • Maintain or improve customer satisfaction • Increase upsell, upgrade, or cross-sell
Other Revenue/Value	• Establish or expand content licensing • Establish or increase content advertisers or sponsors

As another example, I have learned a tremendous amount about the topics and issues content professionals care about from the way they interact with *Content Science Review.* That insight has helped us develop new products, such as Content Science Academy, and more content for the magazine.

PREDICT THE IMPACT OF CHANGES

Explore different scenarios so that you make reasonable estimates instead of wild guesses. The more you understand the other elements, the better you can make such estimates. For instance, the Weather Channel gained enough insight from its "sunny day" launch to not only validate its success but also start predicting what impact that personalizing content even more—not just by weather but also by preferences such as content format (for example, video) and lifestyle—could have on its business.

The ability to predict the impact of changes can be especially useful for moving from a pilot to a larger-scale content effort. For example, I once worked with a niche online retailer of comfort shoes and lower-body health products to pilot offering educational content. We created a microsite on running and injury prevention that included quizzes and articles about running essentials and preventing and treating foot and lower-body health injuries. After reviewing the customer feedback and seeing some uptick in sales for the products featured, the retailer decided to develop a comprehensive set of educational content that ultimately led to a 36 percent increase in weekly sales. If the retailer had not evaluated the pilot and learned from it, the company would not have had enough intelligence to bet on expanding the educational content. And the retailer would have left millions of dollars on the table.

Content intelligence can help you close your information gap and improve the quality of your content decisions. Let's talk more about the impact of quality content decisions.

COMMIT TO QUALITY CONTENT DECISIONS OVER TIME

One of my favorite movies, the critically acclaimed *Casino Royale*, centers on a poker game. The evil and mathematically inclined Le Chiffre arranges a high-rolling, multiday game to win back money he'd lost and now owes to many nefarious characters. In hopes of thwarting Le Chiffre, the British government backs James Bond to buy an entry stake and play the game under cover—a cover that Bond promptly and arrogantly blows. The tension rises over a long series of poker hands, interspersed with attempts to kill Bond on the breaks. (And we think we face decisions under pressure!)

The game has no shortage of entertaining ups and downs. Bond hangs with Le Chiffre at first, winning some hands and minimizing losses on others to amass a stack of chips. More and more players drop out. Bond uses the hands to learn more about Le Chiffre, commenting that the evil mastermind has a "tell." Then, Le Chiffre starts betting even bigger on a particular hand. Bond suspects a bluff and calls it out, to the point that he goes all in on the last bet and shoves all his chips in the pot. Le Chiffre turns over a winning hand. Oops.

Furious, Bond's team attributes his mistake to arrogance. But Bond does not give up. He focuses on what he learned. Le Chiffre faked a bluff, and Bond might have a tell of his own to keep under control. After fending off another attempt on his life, he secures backing from the American government to buy re-entry into the game. Ultimately, Bond wins it by making smarter decisions with the information he gained from the previous rounds and faking a bluff himself.

What does all this have to do with content? A lot, when it comes to making decisions.

Poker experts have criticized details of individual scenes in *Casino Royale*, and I have no doubt those experts are correct. However, what the movie gets right is the impact of trying to make quality decisions again and again (and again and again and again...) so that, over time, you win more than you lose. *Casino Royale* could have simply shown the final hand. But by showing several rounds and hands, the movie reminds us not to focus on winning one big hand. Focus on using the information you have at the start of the game and learning from the outcomes during the game so that when you do face a high-stakes hand, you're more likely to win.

Winning the big hand is an outcome of consistently making quality decisions. Winning is never guaranteed because you cannot control the cards you are dealt and never have all the information available to you. But winning is much, much, *much* more likely when you focus on making the best decisions you can with the available intelligence—the information and insights that you have at the game's start and, this is crucial, that are *added while you're playing the game.*

The same goes for content. If you focus on making quality decisions with the content intelligence you have, over time you will be much more likely to get the outcomes you want. This focus has four implications that might surprise you:

- Evaluate content decisions by decision quality, not outcome.

  In many chapters throughout this book, I tout the importance of understanding the impact and performance of content, such as whether it reaches, engages, and influences the right customers. So you might be shocked for me to say that I don't believe in judging content decisions purely by outcome—whether the content wins or loses. But judging decisions by quality is the only way to learn and acquire the intelligence that can make your future decisions even better.

- Treat content intelligence as a system.

  I've talked about content intelligence as a system because it is not a one-off project. It's an ongoing effort. To inform your ongoing content decisions, you need a steady stream of content data and a regular process from which to glean insight.

- Set expectations with stakeholders—the worthy ones will support you.

  Manage the expectations of your boss and stakeholders by emphasizing the cumulative effect of quality content decisions. Never guarantee overnight results. With many content efforts, it will take at least a year to start seeing winning outcomes.

- Track lessons learned in a center of content excellence.

  You and your team might find it useful to capture lessons learned in a center of content excellence so you can easily consult them in future content decisions. I discuss a center of content excellence in Chapter 11.

Assess Your Readiness for Content Intelligence

Consider these ten questions across the elements of content intelligence as a quick self-assessment. The more you answer yes, the readier your company is to establish and use a content intelligence system.

Element: Data Collection

1. Can your company easily and efficiently evaluate all types of content you offer (for example, thought leadership, sales/sales generation, customer service, technical support)?

2. Does your company collect data or feedback about both your customers' behavior and their perceptions (what people do *and* what people think/perceive) regarding content?

3. Can you and your team easily and quickly access data or feedback about your content's effectiveness and impact?

4. Does your company have a documented plan for content intelligence?

Element: Analysis + Interpretation

5. Can you or your team easily analyze your content-related feedback and data and create reports about your content's effectiveness?

6. Do you have both a detailed (such as team, site, campaign, or even content asset) view and a holistic, company-wide view of your content's impact?

7. Does your company assemble lessons learned from your past data collections, research studies, and testing related to content so that they're easy to share, reference, and apply?

8. Can your company easily compare your content's effectiveness or performance to an industry benchmark of content performance?

Element: Insight + Action

9. Does your team or your company meet regularly to discuss your content's performance or impact, the implications, and potential content decisions?

10. Can you and your team quickly access content best practices, effective examples, and research articles/resources in a center of excellence or similar resource?

CONTENT INTELLIGENCE + QUALITY DECISIONS = CONTENT GENIUS

A genius is someone who is exceptionally intelligent or creative in a particular capacity or field. As business relies more and more on content, we need more content geniuses in the world. You can become one by setting up a system of content intelligence, making quality decisions about content informed by that intelligence, and then learning from the outcomes as you reflect on the quality of the decision. If for some strange reason that sounds easy, it's not. But the benefit is that, over time, content decisions will become easier and more successful for you.

To recap, the key secret to using content intelligence is committing to making quality content decisions over time. Content intelligence will not give you a formula that guarantees results. But when you make the best decisions you can with the content intelligence you have, you will become a content genius—and much more likely to win.

REFERENCES

1 "Netflix Subscriber Growth Tops Expectations" www.wsj.com/articles/ netflix-expands-growth-in-international-markets-1523911999

2 "How Blink Built Its Business with Email Automation" https://mailchimp.com/ resources/marketing-automation-essentials/how-blink-built-its-business-with-email-automation/

3 "Content Intelligence: A Case Study with American Cancer Society," Colleen Jones and Melinda Baker, *Applied Marketing Analytics*, Vol 2, 2 p152–161

4 "Netflix Subscriber Growth Tops Expectations" wsj.com/articles/ netflix-expands-growth-in-international-markets-1523911999

5 "Forecasting What Mobile Users Want," *Content Science Review* https:// review.content-science.com/2017/08/forecasting-what-mobile-users-want-a-sunny-day-strategy-for-any-type-of-weather/

POWER TO SCALE: MATURE CONTENT OPERATIONS

Empower your company to execute successfully.

10 A MODEL OF CONTENT OPERATIONS MATURITY

Choose the roles, processes, and technology that will allow you to implement your content vision and strategy.

IT'S NOT WHAT THE VISION IS; IT'S WHAT THE VISION DOES.

—Peter M. Senge, systems scientist

DO OR DO NOT. THERE IS NO TRY.

—Yoda

You have a content vision and strategy—perhaps even more than one content strategy. You know what kind of effective and influential content you want to offer. You're committed to establishing a system of content intelligence to inform ongoing content decisions. Now, you need to execute. Unfortunately, there is no content fairy ready to wave a magic wand. But there is a growing discipline that I call content operations, and it will help you sustain and even scale your implementation.

WHAT CONTENT OPERATIONS IS

Content operations is the behind-the-scenes work of managing content activities as effectively and efficiently as possible. Today, content operations often require a mix of elements related to people, process, and technology. **Table 10.1** shows a sample.

Table 10.1 Sample Elements in Content Operations

PEOPLE	PROCESS	TECHNOLOGY
Content roles	Content supply chain	Content management
Content responsibilities	Content workflow	Content automation
Company culture	Content localization	Content intelligence
Content leadership	Content governance	Artificial intelligence
Content training	Content templates	Content translation

If this sampling already seems like more operations than you bargained for, you are not alone. Many companies I come across think of content operations as scrambling once each month to get a blog post together, if they think about content operations at all. It is time to think differently about your company's content work.

WHY CARE ABOUT CONTENT OPERATIONS

Amateurs talk strategy; professionals talk logistics, as the saying goes. If you are new to content, your instinct will be to underestimate the effort it takes to sustain and scale effective content. Even if you are not new to content, you are facing unprecedented change, as we discussed in the opening chapters. The demand for content that meets high customer expectations has never been greater. So in a way, we are all new to content and at risk of underestimating what it takes to succeed.

Considering content operations will help align your behind-the-scenes activities with your content vision and strategy so that you reduce the risk of failure and make repeating or scaling success easier. More specifically, considering content operations will help you gain efficiencies and make the most of your content assets by

- Putting the right people in the right roles
- Creating or streamlining processes
- Distinguishing between maintenance and ongoing innovation
- Choosing the technologies and tools with the right features to support your operations

To help companies plan for content operations, I developed a simple maturity model.

A MATURITY MODEL FOR CONTENT OPERATIONS

Statistician George Box once said, "All models are wrong, but some are useful." In that spirit, I developed this maturity model to help companies "get real" about their content operations. The model can help your company identify your current level of content operations and then decide whether that level will support your content vision and strategy. If it doesn't, then the model can help you plan to get to the next level of content operations.

I based this model on

- My experience with in-depth consulting for dozens of companies and training for thousands of content professionals
- Content leadership and operations studies conducted by Content Science, with 200 content professionals participating

So although this model might not be perfectly right, it's informed by enough data and feedback to be useful. The model consists of five levels, as you can see in **Table 10.2**.

Table 10.2 The Five Levels of Content Operations

LEVEL	DESCRIPTION
1. Chaotic	No formal content operations, only ad hoc approaches
2. Piloting	Trying content operations in certain areas, such as for a blog
3. Scaling	Expanding formal content operations across business functions
4. Sustaining	Solidifying and optimizing content operations across business functions
5. Thriving	Sustaining while also innovating and seeing return on investment

In our 2017 study of content operations, 51 percent of participants reported that their companies were at level 3, while only 5 percent of participants reported their companies at level 5[1] (**Figure 10.1**). I believe that our study sample was slightly skewed toward companies that care enough about content to hire content professionals. Based on my experience, I'd put most companies today at levels 2 or 3.

Figure 10.1: Results of a 2017 study of companies self-reporting their content operating levels

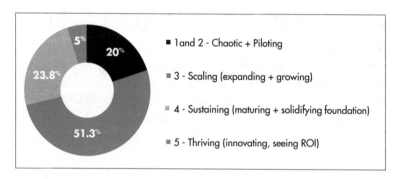

Let's briefly walk through each level of content operations maturity.

LEVEL 1—CHAOTIC: AD HOC APPROACHES

At this level, content for most people is an afterthought. The key characteristics of this level are summarized in **Table 10.3**.

Table 10.3 Chaotic Characteristics

CHARACTERISTIC	DESCRIPTION
People	No content leadership exists.
	Few if any defined and dedicated content roles exist.
	No to little awareness and understanding of content value and issues by stakeholders exist.
Process	No content processes exist.
	If content is needed, it's a last-minute scramble or even an emergency.
	Content is not evaluated, maintained, or governed.
	A change to content is made if there is a complaint or problem.
Technology	Few content considerations for technology decisions exist.
	A content management or marketing automation tool might be present but hasn't been implemented thoughtfully.

LEVEL 2—PILOTING: BRINGING SOME ORDER TO THE CHAOS

At this level, the chaos continues in most areas, but enough people have felt the pain of content chaos or seen the potential of great content that they want to make a change (**Table 10.4**).

Table 10.4 Piloting Characteristics

CHARACTERISTIC	DESCRIPTION
People	Some informal content leadership is emerging.
	Content is becoming part of already existing roles, such as web development, graphic design, or marketing coordination.
	Stakeholders' awareness and understanding of content value and issues are low but growing.
Process	A project plan for the pilot(s) is in place, but there are few or no ongoing content processes.
	Content outside the pilot is not evaluated, maintained, or governed.
	At least one pilot is used as a success story to gain support for more content operations.
	A change to content is made if there is a complaint or problem.

table continues on next page

Table 10.4 Piloting Characteristics *(continued)*

CHARACTERISTIC	DESCRIPTION
Technology	Few content considerations are used for technology decisions.
	A content management or marketing automation tool might be present but hasn't been implemented thoughtfully.

LEVEL 3—SCALING: TRYING TO REPEAT SUCCESS

With the scaling level, a company has experienced at least some success from piloting content operations and wants to expand the content operations (**Table 10.5**).

Table 10.5 Scaling Characteristics

CHARACTERISTIC	DESCRIPTION
People	A formal content leader, often at management level, is defined or hired.
	More distinct content roles are defined or hired, usually related to production, such as writer/editor or content designer.
	Stakeholders' have growing awareness and understanding of content value and issues.
Process	New content efforts get a project plan.
	Content work is integrated into existing processes, such as marketing campaign planning or agile development.
	Additional content processes start to be identified.
	Interest in data to evaluate the impact of content grows.
Technology	Technology changes and new technology decisions start to factor into content.
	Implementation of existing technology and tools changes to better accommodate content work.
	New technology and tools for content work start to be evaluated and purchased.

LEVEL 4—SUSTAINING: CREATING MORE ORDER THAN CHAOS

Companies at this level of content operations are not only establishing content operations for each business function but also aligning them to create a core content capacity (**Table 10.6**).

Table 10.6 Sustaining Characteristics

CHARACTERISTIC	DESCRIPTION
People	An executive is defined or hired as a content leader.
	Content-related managers are defined or hired.
	More distinct content roles are defined or hired related to functions outside production, such as content strategist or content analyst.
	Stakeholders have widespread understanding of content value.
Process	New content efforts get a project plan.
	Content work that is integrated into existing processes is optimized.
	Additional content processes are established and working well.
	Content intelligence is established.
Technology	Technology changes and new technology decisions continue to factor in content requirements or needs.
	Implementation of existing technology and tools is optimized for content work.
	New technology and tools for content work continue to be evaluated and purchased.

LEVEL 5—THRIVING: MAINTAINING ORDER AND SYSTEMATIZING INNOVATION

Companies with thriving content operations are doing everything at level 4, and they have enough resources to fund, ironically, returning to chaos in a controlled way—innovation. These companies devote some operational resources to explore where and how to innovate, and then pilot select innovations and eventually adopt them in core operations (**Table 10.7**).

Table 10.7 Thriving Characteristics

CHARACTERISTIC	DESCRIPTION
People	A chief content officer oversees all content efforts and operations and leads innovation.
	Additional content executives and managers are defined and hired.
	More distinct content roles are defined or hired related to functions outside production, such as content engineer.
	Stakeholders have widespread understanding of content value, though they still might view it as subservient to other capacities or functions.
Process	A process for ongoing content innovation and strategy is established.
	Content work that is integrated into existing processes is optimized.
	Additional content processes are established and working well.
	Content intelligence is used and applied regularly.
Technology	Advanced technology and intelligence are explored as part of content innovation.
	Technology changes and new technology decisions continue to factor into content.
	Implementation of existing technology and tools is optimized for content work.
	New technology and tools for content work continue to be evaluated and purchased.

LARGE COMPANIES MIGHT HAVE MULTIPLE MATURITY LEVELS

If you're a large company or enterprise, you might find that different areas of your company are at different levels of content operations maturity. That's OK. You can use areas of your company that are more mature as models or sources of ideas for less mature areas. You might even be able to share technology and tools so that you can bring maturity across your company in efficient and cost-effective ways.

For example, I once worked with a large telecommunications client that had very different levels of content maturity operations in its business-to-consumer (B2C) functions compared to its business-to-business (B2B) functions. The B2C content teams operated at a solid level 3 and were making progress toward level 4. The teams were in the process of implementing a more sophisticated content management system, automating their workflow, and exploring how to use machine learning to optimize offers. Additionally, B2C teams were even hiring content engineers. However, B2B content teams had built a good rapport with the team and many stakeholders, and they were composed mostly of writers and editors and operated at level 2. The B2B operations had no content management system (really!), low visibility with content stakeholders, and frequent disagreements and miscommunications both within their team and with stakeholders. As the company realized the disparity, I worked with them to facilitate adapting what was working for the B2C teams to the B2B teams as well as to explore the use of the content management system and workflow tools across teams. The conglomerate has continued to make progress in maturing their content operations.

SMALL BUSINESSES CAN MATURE CONTENT OPERATIONS QUICKLY

With operations, small businesses can have a big advantage. Often, small businesses can get to level 3 or 4 much more quickly than a big business because they have less bureaucracy to overcome and more control over the entire customer experience. Burn, the spinning studio I mentioned in earlier chapters, was at level 4 from its start thanks to careful planning of the customer experience. Smart small businesses can also try to optimize solutions faster than larger ones. For example, the Rack Athletic Performance Center has solved the problem of sourcing content in several creative ways, such as

- Forming a reward system where the Rack coaches earn the opportunity to contribute articles to a Knowledge Center. The articles are useful to customers and show the coaches' expertise. Content is something coaches get to do, not something they have to do.

- Profiling the Rack customers as they achieve goals and overcome challenges.

- Integrating into their daily routines the taking and posting of photos and videos that demonstrate exercises, show clients using equipment, and more.

- Encouraging customers to take photos and videos of themselves in action and post them to social media, where the Rack can repost them.

- Automating a set of emails for new customers that orient them to the Rack and connect them to more useful content.

The Rack implemented and optimized these approaches over the course of a few months. A large company would take at least a year to do something comparable.

What's Your Level of Content Operations Maturity?

Want to assess your company's level of content operations maturity? Is your company chaotic, piloting, scaling, sustaining, or thriving? Take the Content Operations Assessment online at content-science.com/contentops to get a quick assessment and a free copy of the latest content operations study.

If you consider your company to be at level 3 or below, you're not alone. In the next chapter, we'll explore how to mature your content operations from your current level to the next level. If you assessed your company as level 4 or 5, the next chapter will help you maintain or increase that level as you scale.

REFERENCES

1   "Content Operations and Leadership Study: Detailed Findings," *Content Science Review*

11 LEAP TO THE NEXT LEVEL OF CONTENT OPERATIONS

• •

Transform content into a core competency sooner, not later.

SOMETIMES, TO CHANGE A SITUATION YOU ARE IN REQUIRES
YOU TO TAKE A GIANT LEAP. BUT YOU WON'T BE ABLE TO
FLY UNLESS YOU ARE WILLING TO TRANSFORM.

—Suzy Kassem, poet and philosopher

ALWAYS IN MOTION IS THE FUTURE.

—Yoda

Aspirations. In my research on content operations, I was happy to find no shortage of aspirations. Even though most study participants reported being at content operations level 3 or lower, the vast majority also reported a desire to reach level 4 (sustain) or level 5 (thrive) (**Figure 11.1**).

Figure 11.1: Most content professionals reported aspirations to mature their content operations[1]

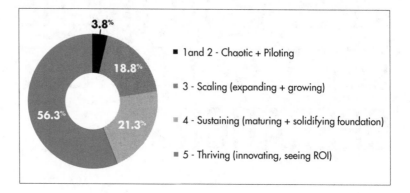

These aspirations for content operations are smart. Why? I believe that every company, big and small, will need content as a core competency that the company can use to its advantage. And right now, creating that competency before your competitors is an advantage unto itself.

MATURE CONTENT OPERATIONS MAKE CONTENT A CORE COMPETENCY

This point bears repeating: *every company will need content as a core competency*. And that competency will frequently cut across business functions, similar to the way competencies like information technology/engineering and design are crucial across business functions such as product, sales, marketing, and support. After observing a wide range of companies and considering the issue carefully for years, I now believe strongly in content as its own competency and that, at ideal maturity, it does not belong in other competencies or functions. Content is not design. Content is not marketing. Content is not information technology or engineering. Content is not support. Content is important to such competencies and functions, but content belongs in content.

If a company does not elevate content to a cohesive core competency, then the company is likely to suffer problems that make content ineffective and that make its operations inefficient at scale. Examples of those problems include but are by no means limited to

- Duplicating efforts on content, from strategy to creation to translation to delivery
- Offering content that is conflicting or inconsistent—or that comes across to customers that way
- Creating content with an inappropriate voice or tone
- Leaving significant gaps between customer needs and your content
- Failing to grow your content capacity and supply chain to meet demand
- Failing to optimize processes to create, deliver, and manage content
- Missing opportunities to learn from and act on content intelligence
- Missing opportunities to innovate your business with content-driven products or services
- Increasing risk of buying duplicate or incompatible content-related technologies and tools

Additionally, content requires unique capabilities, processes, and tools that other competencies and functions do not support well or at all. Examples include but are not limited to

- Mapping content needs to customer journeys
- Exploring and testing concepts for new content to meet customer needs
- Orchestrating a content supply chain
- Developing an editorial approach and managing an editorial calendar
- Producing audio and video, from writing scripts to coordinating talent to shooting film
- Modeling and engineering content for optimal delivery, personalization, and more (see the next section, "Success Factors in Maturing Content Operations")
- Selecting technology and tools to support content operations
- Establishing and using a content intelligence system

Although productive collaboration must happen between content and other business functions, that does not mean that content operations should be scattered throughout other functions. Content operations must be organized and aligned, or else your company will flounder not simply with content but with business itself.

So how can you mature content operations into a core competency? While the exact approach might, and likely will, vary from company to company, I can offer several success factors worth considering.

SUCCESS FACTORS IN MATURING CONTENT OPERATIONS

The Content Science team conducted in-depth analysis of our study participants' answers, both those who reported success and those who reported that their company was at a high level of maturity. I combined those insights with my observations in consulting and training to identify success factors. To leap from your company's current level of content operations to the next level and beyond, closely consider the success factors in these four areas:

- **L**eadership
- **E**xperimentation
- **A**utomation
- **P**eople

Let's start with leadership.

LEADERSHIP

It will be impossible to mature content operations at your company to levels 4 or 5 without leadership. I don't mean leaders who are merely supportive of content. I mean leaders who have content expertise and who focus on making content successful for the company.

Hire a Chief Content Officer Soon

If you or your company are serious about content, I encourage you to hire a chief content officer or similar executive role early because it is the most effective and efficient approach to maturing operations. Once hired, this role can establish vision and strategy and then align and optimize teams, processes, and technologies.

The alternative, especially for a large company, is to wait until after content operations emerge under other business functions, such as sales, support, design, and product. And then you start to experience pain, such as different teams unknowingly creating similar content or turf wars emerging over who is responsible for what content. Your company will likely hire a content executive at that point anyway, and then the content executive has to use time and effort to reset vision and strategy, change teams, fix processes, and revisit decisions before making meaningful progress.

One distinction of the chief content officer role is crystallizing and advocating for a content vision. In my studies with Content Science, vision was far and away the top characteristic reported as effective in a content leader.[2] The person in this role needs to unify the content teams and capabilities under a common vision, advocate for turning that content vision into reality, and lead the team to take ownership of the vision. Noel McDonagh, the director of information development at Dell EMC, articulates the value this way:

> Probably the key thing that enables us to operate as a team is sharing a vision, sharing the plans, and ensuring each individual knows what the vision is and can contribute to it on an ongoing basis.

Another distinction of this role is defining and justifying budget. That might sound obvious, but I was shocked by one of our study findings. Most participants reported not only having operations at level 3 or less but also that they did not know what their company's content budget was. How could this be? We learned from our comments and interviews that, for most participants, budgets didn't work like that. Content was baked into other activities or functions, like marketing or support, but didn't have its own planning, line items, and the like. Jack Lew once said that a budget "is not just a collection of numbers, but an expression of our values and aspirations." The chief content officer puts numbers behind what a company values and aspires to with content.

Empower Content Coaches and Advocates

Mature content operations need more than executive leadership. They need managers, team leaders, or project leaders who are empowered to coach their teams on content issues. And just about everyone on the team must be prepared to advocate for content. Joseph Campo of Dassault Systèmes Solidworks describes the value of getting content buy-in.

> You have to get some sort of buy-in. Bottom line, people need to see what the big-picture vision is, what the goal is, and how they fit into that vision, and either buy in or not. If they don't buy in, then you're gonna have somebody who might leave, or they might just do the minimum possible to get the job done.

Content operations mature more smoothly when each member of the content team is equipped to lead.

EXPERIMENTATION

One of our studies found that companies with maturing content operations were more likely to have at least some elements of content intelligence, even if they didn't yet have an entire system.[3] Chapters 8 and 9 cover content intelligence in depth, but here I want to note two insights that can help you succeed.

Enable Content Genius with Data Access

While they might not call it content genius, companies that are maturing in their content approach are empowering their teams to evaluate their content decisions. Lance Yoder, a program manager at the international health technology company Cerner Corporation, explains what encouraging content genius is like.

> [Our teams are] really strong in analytics—they're able to measure and define variables and recognize different data patterns and how they translate to content.[4]

While analytics are not all you need to make a content decision, they certainly help. Another study participant describes how limited access to analytics and other data hinders content decisions.

> If we could get web analytics to report back who's going where, how often, what they're looking up, and were they successful, that would be

invaluable to us. Unfortunately, the way our IT department has set that up it's very restricted, very broad, and it's almost useless.

A company that forces its content team to make decisions without data will never mature its content operations.

Dedicate Effort to Innovation

Mature companies devote ongoing effort to larger-scale experimentation—in other words, to researching and considering bigger bets on content. As an example, one of our anonymous study participants describes observing companies push the boundaries of content.

> I go to trade shows, and it's hard not to salivate over some organizations and what they've done—these new innovations. It's clear just from what they're doing that these organizations truly invest in their content. They're fully committed to and understand the value of content, and you can see it just in the number of things they're trying, even if some of them fail. I think if that level of understanding or investment is there, companies are able to go a lot further.

As I noted in Chapter 9, exploring ways to innovate paid off for Netflix, and for MailChimp, and it will pay off for you.

Create a Center for Content Excellence

You don't have to call it a center for content excellence—I've seen everything from "Big Book of Knowledge" to "Content Awesome Central." Regardless of what you call it, you need a go-to place to

- Capture key lessons learned about your content so you don't needlessly repeat tests or analyses.

- Summarize new outside research about content to save your teams research time and to spur ideas for optimizing or innovating content.

- Crystallize best practices to help your company maintain a high standard of content.

- Find training resources that can support discussions or briefings with stakeholders.

You can do this in a format that works for your company or team. I've seen everything from a wiki to an intranet portal to a set of Google docs.

AUTOMATION

Companies with maturing content operations look to automation as a crucial factor in making their processes more efficient and scalable. Noel McDonagh of Dell EMC nicely explains the importance of automation in scaling content operations.

> AI and machine learning is the only way we're going to be able to deal with the fact that the demand for content is increasing exponentially. We're going to have to automate the production of certain aspects of content.

Such companies are

- Embracing automation of content workflow, including how content moves from a draft state to a final published state
- Exploring automation of content optimization, such as multivariate testing, where different versions of content are tested for impact or performance
- Modeling content, such as defining content components and content types, to support personalized and multichannel delivery
- Trying artificial intelligence and machine learning to do everything from accelerating content optimization to actually creating content

One thing I love about content automation is that it benefits successful companies large and small alike. While their scale might differ, the need to respond to the intense customer demand for content is the same. And suitable technology is available for companies of all sizes. For a sample, see Appendix C, "Resources."

PEOPLE

Although automation can address a range of content tasks for maturing content operations, automation doesn't replace people. Consider the following success factors.

Cultivate a Culture System

Culture is the often-overlooked but powerful connective tissue in content operations. Positive culture forms a level of trust that reduces the need for documenting and implementing pedantic rules and excessive reviews. Culture also makes governance infinitely smoother. I find that companies that already have a strong progressive culture create the right content culture more easily. But even if your company lacks culture, you can create a system that cultivates strong culture for your content operations.

Give Permission to Fail (but Learn)

Planning, producing, and delivering effective content requires people to put their minds and even their hearts "out there." Oftentimes it works; sometimes it does not. Instead of chastising people for failing, encourage people to embrace curiosity and problem-solving. This approach fosters deep trust that is crucial to your success. Ann Marie Gray, who directed content marketing at Morningstar Financial for years and is currently the vice president of content at Americas' SAP Users Group, explains:

> Having a "safe space" for critically examining our work is essential. People on content teams need to trust their colleagues, share their work, and share honest feedback. Leaders need to create and maintain an environment where that can happen by establishing expectations about showing each other respect and kindness.

Encouraging content genius, as I mentioned, further reinforces this notion of learning from, instead of harshly judging, content efforts.

Don't Hire a Rock Star; Hire a Star Constellation

Your content operations will not be sustainable or scalable if they depend on one content rock star. That star will flame out quickly. Instead, you need to assemble a constellation of stars who, together, can make your content operations shine. In our "What Makes Content Teams Thrive?" study, we asked content leaders about the qualities they look for in hiring new team members. Top answers included

- High performing
- Curious
- Systems thinking
- Considerate
- Competent in a content skill or role

I have found particularly useful two insights shared with me by content leaders. Tracy V. Wilson, of the immensely successful HowStuffWorks, notes

> I look for overachievers [when hiring], regardless of the role they are looking for—people who are driven to do exceptionally well.

Aaron Burgess, of the high-potential company HomeAway, explains how the mix of qualities enlightens content operations:

> There are some intangible qualities that team members need to have: curiosity, tenacity, systems thinkers, design thinkers. People who can look at a complex problem and break it down into simpler elements, synthesize information, make sense of lots of user data and product requirements, and consistently ask "why?" and then get from "why?" to a better way of doing things.

If you are a content team of one for now, you can still connect with other stars through conferences, training, and online communities so that your content efforts shine bright.

Hire for New Roles

By now, I hope it's clear that hiring a writer/editor (or dozens of writer/editors) will probably not give you the capabilities you need. Consider hiring people who can take on a variety of content roles, including the five emerging roles in **Table 11.1**.

Table 11.1 Emerging Content Roles

ROLE	DESCRIPTION
Content strategist	Identifies key content opportunities and conducts high-level planning
Content analyst	Establishes or refines content intelligence systems and conducts analyses or evaluations
Content engineer	Models content and architect rules to enable dynamic, automated content delivery and management
Content designer	Plans and develops the content for specific experiences, especially dynamic experiences and conversational interfaces
Content marketer	Plans and coordinates editorial and production for marketing

A small or medium-sized company might need someone to take on more than one of these roles, such as content strategist and content analyst. A large company often needs these roles to remain distinct, and their demand for these roles is increasing. As of this writing, each of these roles represents hundreds of full-time position openings on career sites such as Indeed.com.

Train, Train, Train, and Train Some More

If you already have writer/editors or other content professionals on your team, you might need to train them in new or additional roles. Our studies have found that companies with maturing content operations offer training opportunities specific to content for their content teams. Simply offering the training reinforces the other success factors because it conveys that the company takes content seriously, embraces experimentation, and supports curiosity. To make the most of experimentation and automation, modern content roles need technology savvy, which demands training. Product content manager Erin Crews of MailChimp elaborates:

> We started by establishing our content team's mission and clarifying roles and career paths for both individual contributors and managers. Setting clear expectations for content roles early on helped us identify skill gaps on our team and find training or other resources to fill them. We've drawn on a mix of in-house workshops, conferences and seminars, and learnings from our design team's critique process.

One reason I started Content Science Academy was to provide cost-effective content-specific training in a convenient online format. Many content-related technology companies have their own training resources, as well, at reasonable cost. For a sample, see Appendix C, "Resources."

CONSIDER A CONTENT OPERATIONS ROADMAP

By now, you should have a sense of where your company falls in its level of content maturity and some ideas about what to do to take your company to the next level. Overwhelmed? Not sure where to start for your company? Creating a content operations roadmap can help. You can think through issues such as

- What changes can I make right away?
- What changes are feasible in the short term?

- What changes will take more effort and planning for the long term?
- What support do I need and from which executives and stakeholders?

This roadmap can take a variety of formats. I like to use a visual format, as shown in **Figure 11.2**, to support presentations and discussions. A spreadsheet or other document can complement that visual with more detail as you refine your plans.

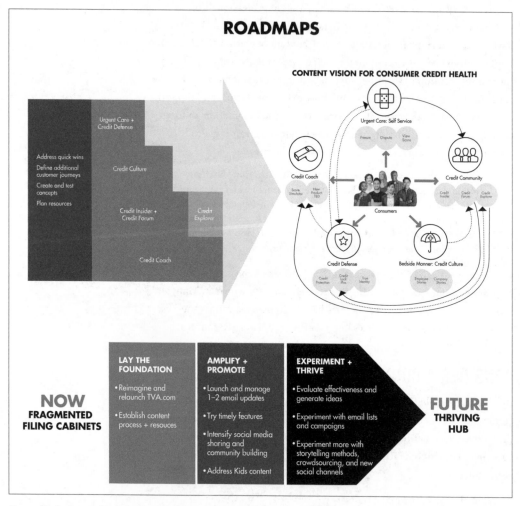

Figure 11.2: A sample content operations roadmap illustrating high-level phases of change

Congratulations. In reaching this point in *The Content Advantage*, you have closely considered content, from vision through implementation. Before we conclude, I ask you to consider one more aspect of content: the future.

REFERENCES

1 "Content Operations and Leadership Study: Detailed Findings," Content Science

2 "What Makes Content Teams Thrive?" Content Science

3 "Content Operations and Leadership Study: Detailed Findings," Content Science

4 "What Makes Content Teams Thrive?" Content Science

PRESCIENCE: THE CONTENT FUTURE

Consider the imminent and prepare for the unknown.

12 ROBOTS, RELATIONSHIPS, AND RESPONSIBILITY

• •

The content future will be anything but boring.

WE CAN'T CONTROL SYSTEMS OR FIGURE THEM OUT. BUT WE CAN DANCE WITH THEM!
—Donella H. Meadows, *Thinking in Systems*

WELL, IF DROIDS COULD THINK, THERE'D BE NONE OF US HERE, WOULD THERE?
—Obi-Wan Kenobi

At the start of this book, we established that content will make or break businesses as they undergo digital transformation—and digital transformation will only accelerate in the future. So you can count on content's importance growing. But beyond that, what does the future of content hold? I offer my humble answer as you consider how to make content an advantage to your company. I see the content future as coming down to three Ss—small, systems, and soul.

THE CONTENT FUTURE IS SMALL (AND MIDSIZE)

Although I have worked for and with ginormous companies, I believe more and more that the future of content lies with small and midsize businesses because of two factors: effort to change and technology access.

EFFORT TO CHANGE

Small and midsize businesses (SMBs) often have less of a legacy mindset, and often have fewer bureaucratic processes, outdated roles, and old ways of working that they need to change. Instead of putting time and resources into extensive change management, SMBs can make repeated small changes over time or simply establish the right vision, strategy, and operations at the start, then optimize them as needed.

For example, I had the pleasure of working with one of the largest, oldest, and most prestigious nonprofits in the United States. This enterprise suffered from a print mindset that held back its capacity to deliver the right content at the right time across touchpoints such as the web. It was not until the retirement of the director clinging to that mindset that the organization felt free to start modernizing its approach to content. Once started, the effort took several years. These kinds of barriers to change happen in prestigious corporate enterprises as well. It's not hard to see the nimble advantage an SMB has in embracing and executing modern content approaches.

TECHNOLOGY ACCESS

The technology available to SMBs is getting significantly better, and I predict this improvement will accelerate. Why? One factor is that there are many, many, many, many more SMBs than enterprises in the world. The market is big, and it's getting bigger as more and more people start side businesses or go out on their own in the gig economy. Another factor? Selling new technology solutions to enterprises is about as easy as convincing Darth Vader to leave the dark side. The selling process is often slow and increasingly complicated as more departments become involved in the decision. Technology to support marketing automation, for example, has to involve not only procurement and information technology but also the marketing department. Consequently, technology companies are figuring out how to offer more sophisticated solutions for SMBs and profit because of the quick sales and high customer volume. SMBs can now very affordably get the quality technology that is important for content—such as email and marketing automation, customer relationship management, content management, analytics, and digital asset management—and can acquire features that are as good as or better than enterprise solutions. I don't foresee that trend stopping any time soon. (For examples of this technology, see Appendix C.)

I also believe that SMBs have an advantage with soul, as we'll soon cover. For now, I'll reiterate that the content future will reward agility. What else will the content future reward? Systems thinking.

THE CONTENT FUTURE IS SYSTEMS

When you buy chicken, veggies, or even frozen burritos (guilty!) at the grocery store or market, you're not simply filling your cart. You're participating in a complicated food system. Think about all the people, processes, and technology that go into the farming, distribution, marketing, and more so that you can buy your food. In the same way, when your customers view a video on your website, they are consuming the result of a complex content system. Think about the people, processes, and technology behind the planning, production, and delivery of an effective video. Companies that view doing content well as a system (or, perhaps more accurately, as a collection of interdependent systems) will be well equipped for the future. While I can't be sure about everything the future holds, I am certain there are no magical content fairies.

So what exactly do I mean by system? I prefer Donella Meadows' flexible definition:

> A system is a set of things—people, cells, molecules, or whatever—interconnected in such a way that they produce their own pattern of behavior over time.[1]

This book has described a set of content "things" that you can connect *now* to produce a pattern of behavior for your company *over time*. Your content vision and strategy describe the behavior you want. Your operations connect systems such as

- Content supply chain
- Content intelligence
- Content delivery
- Business competency (design, and so on)
- Business function (marketing, support, and so on)

Figure 12.1 offers an example of visualizing the high-level connection between a number of systems at a conglomerate. This systems view helps anticipate or correct problems and respond to new needs. In the case of this conglomerate, diagramming the system helped the teams involved identify and communicate changes such as involving content early in the planning process and unlocking access to the necessary data.

What is the biggest change to these systems in the future? The rise of machines that take on roles that used to be exclusively people roles. More and more content-related technologies will write text (also called natural language generation), personalize content delivery in touchpoints ranging from websites to chatbots, and combine those capabilities into completely automated content optimization. In **Figure 12.2**, I summarize how this can work right now if you have the right customer data, content intelligence, and content management system. (For more details, see Appendix C.)

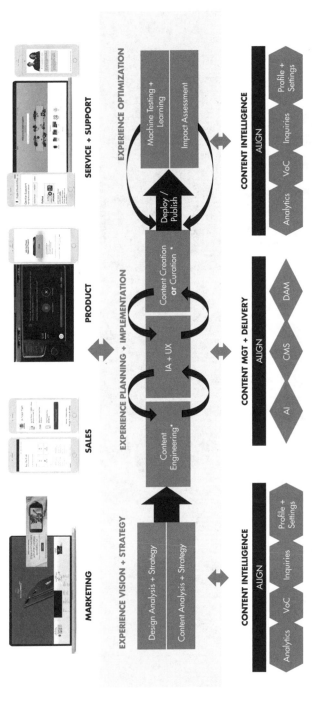

Figure 12.1: A systems view of content at a large conglomerate

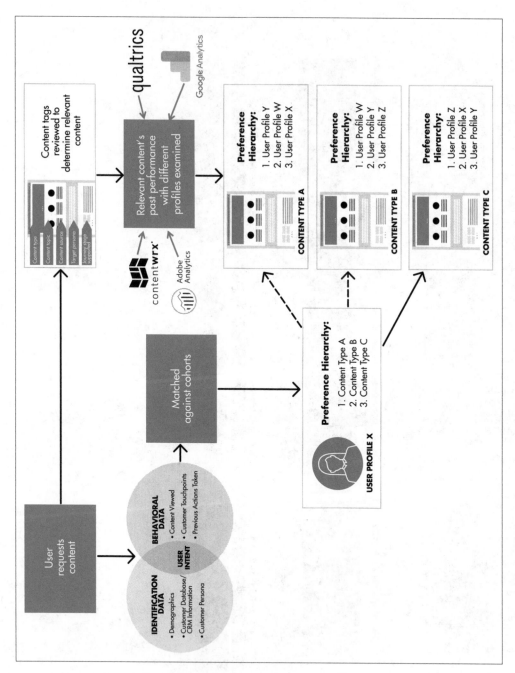

Figure 12.2: How content intelligence and machine learning automate content delivery and optimization

Companies can make much of this future happen now, so why don't more of them do so? Because they don't have the right people in place to teach the machines about content. Companies need to move people to different roles, especially the roles of content analyst, content strategist, and content engineer discussed in Chapter 11. **Figure 12.3** illustrates a shift in roles that I recommend to an enterprise committed to making better use of content technology. For you, the balance of roles might be different. The point is that if you add different machines to your content system, be prepared to change the way people work in your content system too.

I'm only scratching the surface of the capabilities of the machines. I have no doubt technology will be able to do much more for content in the future. No matter what those capabilities are, companies that view content as a system will be better able to accommodate the machine capabilities and shift the roles of people to make the most of those capabilities.

The content future will demand systems in which machines play a crucial role. But we can't forget the human side of content.

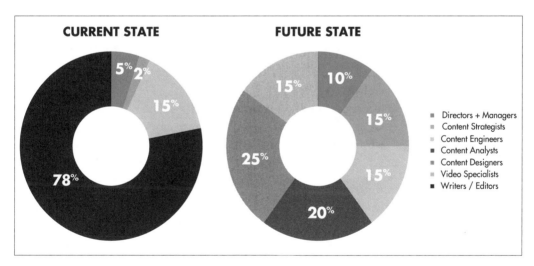

Figure 12.3: An example of a shift in roles

THE CONTENT FUTURE IS SOUL

One of the discoveries from Content Science's ContentWRX software that surprised me most was the need for richer content.[2] We have no shortage of content on the interwebs. But that content is often too basic or superficial to satisfy people's needs. Additionally, evidence is already mounting that Generation Z is bored by the Internet. Turns out that seeing the same meme or covering the same topic again and again and again isn't cutting it with the generation growing up with constant connection to content.[3]

This lack of depth and spark is a huge opportunity for companies who dare to bare their soul and listen to customers bare theirs. And I believe that small and midsize businesses are in the best position to take advantage because of their close connection to a calling and to their customers.

CONNECTION TO CALLING

SMBs often have their founders still involved in the company and, consequently, constant reminders of *why* the company was founded. Bain & Company strategy consultants Chris Zook and James Allen refer to this as the founder's mentality and note in their excellent book of the same name that companies whose founders are still involved perform 3.1 times better than other companies. Zook and Allen convincingly argue that the problems experienced by most floundering companies—their examples focus on large companies such as Charles Schwab—can be traced back to losing connection with the founder's mentality.[4] This mentality is the real purpose, calling, or "why" behind the company's existence. For Charles Schwab, that "why" was to give small but competent investors a brokerage that opened up an investing world previously dominated by large investors.

I find this mentality invaluable to efficiently crafting and maintaining a vision, a voice, themes, topics, and more for content. For instance, the company Method, featured in this book's first edition, has expanded from cleaning products to a variety of products for the home. Yet the founders' story and voice still permeates the content, from the website to the blog to the product packaging. The founders' original mission to fight all things dirty is undeniably clear and compelling.

Zook and Allen point out that Charles Schwab lost its way as the company grew and after Charles Schwab left, then regained success when he returned. The author duo goes on to offer ways for large companies to scale the founder's mentality without the founder being present. That is certainly better than doing nothing. But it is more change to manage, and we know how well many enterprises manage change (see the section "The Content Future Is Small [and Midsize]"). To me, this insight about enterprises losing connection to their calling underscores another big advantage for SMBs.

CONNECTION TO CUSTOMERS

SMBs are often closer to their customers than enterprises are, so SMBs can more efficiently and accurately assess their customers' needs across the journey and evaluate the impact of content. Large companies often have many layers of separation between executives and the people interacting with their customers, making it easier for executives to ignore customer feedback and harder for executives who do want that feedback to get it in a timely and actionable way. As well, enterprises usually have different departments affecting different stages of the customer journey, from marketing to sales to product to support. With that complexity, of course, comes internal politics. As one simple example, a director for a B2B solution at a conglomerate I worked with insisted to the content team that they use a particular word despite evidence that the word confused B2B customers. Instead of listening to customer feedback or trusting the expertise of the content team, he was willing to fall on his sword and die for one word. You can imagine the time-consuming calls and email threads as well as the demotivating bad feelings conjured in the process of deciding about only one word. How much more difficult is it for enterprises to make decisions about entire sentences, paragraphs, videos, visuals, and other content that will meet their customers' needs?

With a close connection to customers, small and midsize businesses are better equipped to offer content with soul. Content with soul won't be simply what survived an internal political battle. It also won't be merely effective and influential, as we discussed in Chapters 6 and 7. Content with soul will seem fresh by introducing nuance, sharing a different viewpoint, or exploring another side of an experience. For instance, REI has expanded its educational content, such as how to prepare for a hike, to include documentaries that uniquely educate and entertain. These documentaries bring a perspective that taps into the values REI shares with its customers, such as environmental stewardship, outdoor adventure, and women's equality. The documentary *Within Reach*, for example, explores the obstacles women are overcoming to gain respect in the world of climbing. REI's documentaries remind me of ESPN's *30 for 30* films about traditional sports or Red Bull's movies about extreme sports, but with a focus and viewpoint designed for REI's customers. Whether you climb or not, if you share in REI's values, you will likely find *Within Reach* compelling. It does not simply educate; it inspires.

Companies that thrive in the future will offer content with soul by deepening their connection to their calling and to their customers, and this connection will likely be yet another advantage for small and midsize businesses.

WHAT THE CONTENT FUTURE MEANS FOR US

The future of content is small, systems, and soul. I believe in this future so much that I decided to place a big bet on it. In the course of writing this edition, I accepted a generous offer from the stellar team at MailChimp to become the head of content. The highly respected business magazine *Inc.* selected this email and marketing automation powerhouse as Company of the Year in 2017.[5] At $525 million in revenue and growing, MailChimp is a midsize company that isn't monkeying around. I'm particularly impressed with its carefully cultivated culture and content passion. What's more, MailChimp customers are small businesses eager to make their email and marketing succeed—and that takes content. I'm ecstatic to make content an advantage not only for MailChimp but also for its millions of enthusiastic small business customers. As a small business owner myself, I have tremendous empathy for what it takes to start and grow a business. And I'm grateful to take on this role while maintaining the products ContentWRX, Content Science Academy, and *Content Science Review*.

Now let's return to the crossroads your company faces. I applaud you for considering a commitment to content. My hope is that our walk through the science of succeeding at content will inform your decision—hopefully, your first of many decisions as an emerging content genius. You can choose to ignore content and hope to survive digital transformation. Or you can choose to do content well and work to thrive. When you make your content make a difference to your customers and to your company, you make your content an advantage.

REFERENCES

1 "Thinking in Systems," Donella Meadows

2 "Content Relevance and Usefulness: Why You Need It and 4 Ways to Achieve It," https://review.content-science.com/2017/10/content-relevance-and-usefulness-why-you-need-it-and-4-ways-to-achieve-it/

3 "Generation Z Is Already Bored by the Internet," www.thedailybeast.com/generation-z-is-already-bored-by-the-internet

4 *The Founder's Mentality*, Chris Zook and James Allen

5 "Want Proof That Patience Pays Off? Ask the Founders of This $525 Million Email Empire," www.inc.com/magazine/201802/mailchimp-company-of-the-year-2017.html

A MORE INFLUENTIAL CONTENT PRINCIPLES

• •

This appendix summarizes more principles of influential content and gives example techniques.

REPETITION THAT DOESN'T BORE OR BROADCAST

The ancient Greeks crafted creative ways of repeating ideas. Why go to such pains? Those toga-sporting orators knew that repetition helps people remember—but also risks boring them. Today, when we use tweets, emails, and ads to blast a message again, again, again, again, again, and *again*, our users could tune us out. So let's take a closer look at repetition.

THREE REALLY IS A CHARM

When it comes to making the same point, three times is enough. Research everywhere, from speech communication to television advertising, suggests three as the magic number. A challenge with web content is that we can't control exactly how many times a user sees or hears our message. But we *can* control how often we publish the same message, how often we change the message, and how we bring the message to life through web content. We can avoid bombarding our users.

APPLY REPETITION TO CONTENT

With web content and some help from modern media, we have the power to plan our repetition wisely.

Editorial Calendar

An editorial calendar is a tool, borrowed from journalism, for planning content over time. Usually a spreadsheet or table, its exact form doesn't matter as much as the planning. When you decide in detail *what* content you will publish and *when*, you're more likely to repeat messages, topics, and themes appropriately.

For tools with editorial calendar–inspired features, see Appendix C.

Hook

In journalism slang, *hook* refers to why content is relevant at a particular time. A hook can help you breathe new life into your message, theme, or topic. Some examples include tying content to

- The season
- An anniversary
- A recognition, such as becoming first, most, or best
- A current event or an industry trend

Amplification

Amplification refers to all the ways to amplify, or enhance, your point instead of repeating it like a robot. For example, on the television show *Northern Exposure*, the poetic disc jockey Chris Stevens used amplification to explain the meaning of light:

> Goethe's final words: "More light." Ever since we crawled out of that primordial slime, that's been our unifying cry: "More light." Sunlight. Torchlight. Candlelight. Neon. Incandescent. Lights that banish the darkness from our caves, to illuminate our roads, the insides of our refrigerators. Big floods for the night games at Soldier Field. Little tiny flashlights for those books we read under the covers when we're supposed to be asleep. Light is more than watts and foot-candles. Light is metaphor.

Classic rhetoricians used words to intensify a point. Today, we can augment an idea through web content in several ways.

Content Formats and Types

We can make points through a combination of photos, podcasts, videos, articles, and more. HowStuffWorks, for example, offers several ways to experience the danger of sharks, especially during *Shark Week*.

Echo

Echo is the social networking phenomenon of other people sharing or restating your message or content. When that happens, you don't have to state it yourself so often. (An extreme version of this is having something go "viral.") A case in point is when MailChimp announced its stance on hate speech on social media in 2017—followers shared the announcement and repeated key points about it.

Three Devices for Repeating Words Remarkably

The ancient Greeks had all kinds of devices for repeating words. Consider these three for emphasis.

1. **Anaphora.** Repeating a word or phrase at the beginning of each clause. Content attracts people. Content motivates people. Content guides people.

2. **Antistasis.** Repetition of a word in a different or contrary sense. Don't be content with your lackluster content.

3. **Diacope.** Repetition of a word or phrase broken up by one or more intervening words. Content, content, content—where will we get the content?

THE OPPORTUNE MOMENT!

Time. A concept so complex that the Greeks had not one but two words for it. *Chronos* meant chronological time, such as morning, noon, and night. *Kairos* meant the opportune moment. It's the *right time* to say something in the *right way*. I think of it as the ideal time to ask people to change their viewpoint or take an action. The key is to ask when people are ready.

DON'T ASK TOO MUCH TOO SOON OR TOO OFTEN

Ancient rhetoricians felt that the opportune moment was special. It didn't come along every day. That's worth remembering when we're tempted to press users quickly for personal information or bombard them with emails, alerts, and tweets.

ASK CLEARLY—AND MAKE ASKING EASY

People won't respond how you'd like if they aren't sure what you want.

At the same time, you have to make asking questions or giving commands easy for your customers in chatbots and voice command interfaces.

REACT TO A CRISIS PROMPTLY AND APPROPRIATELY

A hurricane strikes. A CEO resigns. A damaging video goes viral. Sometimes, the opportune moment arises because of a shocking event. It's much better to say something trustworthy sooner, not later, so people don't panic or spread rumors.

At other times, the opportune moment happens because of a personal crisis or your customers' experience. For instance, companies in financial services, credit monitoring, and health industries often find themselves responding to customers having emergencies ranging from identity theft to illness. Many such companies lack empathy for customers in crisis and blow the opportunity to help, so handling the situation well is an opportunity for your company to differentiate. In this situation, you must speak even more simply and clearly than normal. Why? The emotions your customers experience under stress hijack their brains. The cognitive load makes even simple instructions and tasks much harder.

You also must avoid appearing to take advantage of the situation. As I mention in earlier chapters, I've seen more than one credit monitoring company insist on selling to customers in identity theft crisis instead of helping now and earning the opportunity to sell later. It's no wonder that so many people hate those companies.

APPLY THE OPPORTUNE MOMENT TO CONTENT

On the web, our content can seize *kairos* in several ways.

Advertisement

Chapter 1 noted how ads annoy people. What if ads were more relevant to a website's topics and users? For example, *National Geographic*'s readers typically care about the environment. An IBM ad in the magazine stays pertinent with the message to "build a smarter planet."

However, the desire for relevance can go too far. The pressure to make advertising relevant and impactful has led to conflicts with privacy, especially on search engines and social media sites. I expect this tension to continue and the backlash against invasive advertising to gain momentum. Advertising can be one effective way to influence your customers, but it should not be the only way.

Merchandise-Related Offerings or Content

When customers express strong interest in a topic, product, or service, you have an opportunity to expose those customers to more of what interests them. Amazon, of course, has mastered offering related products to cross-sell, upsell, or repeat sales. The same idea works well for content. *Harvard Business Review*, Netflix, and Red Bull all make discovering related content easy. Never let an interested customer experience a dead end.

Call to Action

Clear, concise, and earnest—what makes a good call to action. The call to action helps in every phase of the customer experience, from encouraging a sale to keeping a customer who was tempted to leave to deepening engagement with a product. As an avid user of the Fitbit system, I find myself responding to calls to action on my watch, on the mobile application, and on the website. These calls range from "You have 124 steps left this hour! Get moving!" to "Are you feeling well rested or a bit sleepy? Check out your sleeping stats."

Chat and Voice Command

Chatbots are all over the place, with 100,000 on Facebook alone.[1] Sales of voice interfaces, such as home assistants Alexa, Home, and Homepod, continue to grow. Consider whether your company needs to develop or join these touchpoints where customers ask the questions and give the commands. If you have a product distributed on Amazon, for example, and your customers can't easily ask Alexa to add it to their shopping lists, you're in trouble. In these touchpoints, being ready for the opportune moment means anticipating the questions and words customers will likely use in context. All the analysis we discussed in Chapter 4 will help.

Instructional Microcopy

Sometimes, helping people act requires more than a well-labeled button. In that case, contextual instructions or help come to the rescue. TurboTax, Capital One, and 23andMe all offer excellent examples throughout their web and mobile experiences.

I am particularly impressed with the way 23andMe offers clear instructions throughout the experience, from signing up on the website to using the package to provide your DNA sample to accessing results on the mobile application. The process is precise and the results are complex, yet the instructional microcopy offers clarity and reassurance in a personable tone. Additionally, the contextual instructions often link to more details for curious customers, and these details concisely but clearly offer more explanation. When I sought more information about my Neanderthal DNA, for example, I learned it might partially explain my high forehead and other physical traits.

Crisis Response

How can you respond aptly? By planning for crisis situations. You can't always prepare for the exact crisis, but you can think of possible crises and have a plan that answers questions like these:

- Where will we publish a response?
- Who should write and approve a response?
- If we need extra people to help us monitor and respond to questions on social networking, how will we get those people?

- What are examples of a good response?
- What style of response is appropriate for our users and our brand?

The CDC responds in a different style to a different crisis—a salmonella outbreak in eggs. A no-nonsense daily summary explains the latest status and what people should do about it.

REFERENCES

1 "Facebook Messenger Hits 100,000 Bots," VentureBeat https://venturebeat.
com/2017/04/18/facebook-messenger-hits-100000-bots/

B INSIGHTS FROM CONTENT GENIUSES

• •

This appendix highlights useful insights from content geniuses around the world who have contributed to *Content Science Review*, participated in a Content Science study, or offered comments on *The Content Advantage* chapters.

CONTENT INTELLIGENCE

[A]nalytics create a feedback loop that allows writers and publishers to hone what resonates with their readers. It gives them insights into not only the content, but the style, language, voice, and even the frequency of creation that their audience desires.[1]

—Alan Segal, vice president of analytics and audience development at CNN

Page views are a fluctuating number that depend on a lot of different factors, and I think that people can get a little too caught up in an arbitrary page view number or an arbitrary return visit number. That has to connect to something—such as how much revenue are you getting based on this.[2]

—Tracy Wilson, editorial director at HowStuffWorks.com

In a world where customer experience is everything, creating the right content is a high-value activity, and using data and feedback to support decision-making about what content to invest in only makes sense.[3]

> —Cathy Ewaschuk, content strategist in information design and development at Dell

CONTENT GOVERNANCE

Fundamentally, governance brings order in a world full of chaos— something every organization can benefit from.[4]

> —Scott Rosenberg, senior director of global marketing operations and governance at Visa

CONTENT LEADERSHIP AND CHANGE

"It's not necessary to change. Survival is not mandatory." This quote from W. Edwards Deming is very Darwinian. Change, adapt, and survive. Or don't. There's no middle ground. That's true whether you're leading a content team, a Fortune 500 enterprise, a small business, or anything in between.[5]

> —Cory Bennett, associate director of user experience at AT&T

When we all feel listened to and appreciated we're more open to accept other ideas around us. Content strategy is exploding all over our bank content teams, and it's because I'm doing the work upfront to get out of the way.[6]

> —Michaela Hackner, head of UX content strategy at Morningstar Financial

CONTENT OPERATIONS AND PROCESSES

In the context of a large organization, when you start looking at content from a client journey and ecosystem perspective, you're immediately faced with technology, people, process, and culture silos. Busting those silos is essential to defining a real end-to-end customer experience through content.[7]

> —Marie Girard, content strategist at IBM

If you want to make a design system your entire team can use, a system that thoughtfully guides the work your team is doing, shouldn't content be a part of it?[8]

> —Michael Haggerty-Villa, principal content designer and strategist
> at Intuit

CONTENT STRATEGY

The stakeholders used to say, "This is what we want to tell people." But if the content fails to match what your audience wants, they won't find it.[9]

> —Melinda Baker, director of web marketing at the American
> Cancer Society

If your strategy-less digital experience, piece of content, or product wore a name tag, what would it say? Would everyone in your organization write the same name on it? What about your users? If not, seize the opportunity to clarify.[10]

> —Laura Jarrell, content strategist at CFA Institute

If a piece of content is published on the internet and no one reads it, does it make a sound? Yes, definitely—and the sound is your CEO's voice saying, What does this content team really do here, anyway?[11]

> —Margaret Magnarelli, vice president of marketing at Monster.com

CONTENT SYSTEMS

Content should be created for purpose rather than placement. That way, the content can be quickly and easily repurposed across brands, hotels, and channels, delivering a consistent experience for customers no matter what channels are selected.[12]

> —David Henderson, director of content operations and localization
> at Hilton

REFERENCES

1 Segal, Alan, "3 Observations on How Analytics Influence Content Creation + Selection at Cox Media Group," *Content Science Review*, November 5, 2015, https://review.content-science.com/2015/11/3-observations-on-how-analytics-influence-content-creation-and-selection-at-cox-media-group/

2 Wilson, Tracy, "How Leading Content Teams Works at HowStuff Works: A Q&A," *Content Science Review*, January 5, 2016, https://review.content-science.com/2016/01/how-leading-content-teams-works-at-howstuffworks-com-a-qa/

3 Ewaschuk, Cathy, "Using Customer Feedback in Content Strategy: Wring your Data for All Its Worth," *Content Science Review*, May 15, 2018, https://review.content-science.com/2018/05/using-customer-feedback-in-content-strategy-wring-your-data-for-all-its-worth/

4 Rosenberg, Scott, "Intel Addresses Modern Marketing Challenges Through Digital Governance," *Content Science Review*, October 11, 2016, https://review.content-science.com/2016/10/intel-addresses-modern-marketing-challenges-through-digital-governance/

5 Bennett, Cory, "Survival Isn't Mandatory: Leading Content Teams During Change," *Content Science Review*, November 15, 2017, https://review.content-science.com/2017/11/leading-content-teams-through-times-of-change/

6 Hackner, Michaela, "Navigating Professional Ambiguity: Leading with Content in the Face of Change at Capital One," *Content Science Review*, May 17, 2016, https://review.content-science.com/2016/05/leading-with-content-in-the-face-of-change-at-capital-one/

7 Girard, Marie, "Raiders of the Lost Content: Silo-busting Adventures in the Corporate Jungle," *Content Science Review*, April 6, 2017, https://review.content-science.com/2017/04/raiders-of-the-lost-content-silo-busting-adventures-in-the-corporate-jungle/

8 Haggerty-Villa, Michael, "Content: The Next Big Thing for Design Systems," *Content Science Review*, May 3, 2018, https://review.content-science.com/2018/05/content-the-next-big-thing-for-design-systems/

9 Baker, Melinda, "Implementing Content Strategy at American Cancer Society," *Content Science Review*, May 1, 2014, https://review.content-science.com/2014/05/implementing-content-strategy-at-american-cancer-society/

10 Jarrell, Laura, "Classified Information: How to Uncover Unseen Content Strategy," *Content Science Review*, September 21, 2017, https://review.content-science.com/2017/09/classified-information-how-to-uncover-unseen-content-strategy/

11 Magnarelli, Margaret, "The 'How? Now. Wow!' Framework That's Helped Monster Supercharge Its Content KPIs," *Content Science Review*, October 26, 2016, https://review.content-science.com/2016/10/the-how-now-wow-framework-thats-helped-monster-supercharge-its-content-kpis/

12 Henderson, David, "The Challenges of Moving to Decoupled Omnichannel Content at Hilton," *Content Science Review*, March 13, 2018, https://review.content-science.com/2018/03/the-challenges-of-moving-to-decoupled-omnichannel-content-at-hilton/

C RESOURCES

• •

This appendix lists resources mentioned throughout the book as well as others that will help you make your content an advantage. I have included resources offered by Content Science, MailChimp, as well as by other companies and organizations I trust.

TECHNOLOGIES + TOOLS

Consider these technologies and tools for planning, creating, delivering, and evaluating your content. Whether you're a small or medium business (SMB) or a large enterprise, there are tools ready to help. The landscape of technologies and tools does change, so do your own research to ensure you consider the latest options.

CONTENT MANAGEMENT + DISTRIBUTION

TOOL/TECHNOLOGY	DESCRIPTION	SMB?	ENTERPRISE?
Drupal	Drupal is an open-source content management platform powering millions of websites and applications.	X	X
Sitecore Web Experience Manager	Sitecore Web Experience Manager CMS is a comprehensive platform powering more than 32,000 websites.		X
Adobe Experience Manager	Adobe Experience Manager helps you create, manage, and optimize digital customer experiences across every channel, including web, mobile apps, digital forms, and communities.		X
Acquia	Acquia offers preconfigured, expertly curated versions of Drupal with one-click installers and packaged solutions.	X	X
Oracle WebCenter Content	Oracle WebCenter is a user engagement platform for social business, connecting people and information.		X
IBM Web Content Manager	IBM Web Content Manager accelerates digital content development and deployment across various web and mobile channels. This comprehensive web management system lets you create, manage, and publish content for different audiences.		X
Episerver CMS	Episerver CMS allows you to manage content seamlessly across screens and channels.	X	X
BloomReach Hippo CMS	BloomReach uses Big Data to capture online demand across channels with relevant user experiences.		X
WordPress	WordPress.org is a simple, easy to use web software you can use to create a beautiful website or blog.	X	X
Sitefinity	Sitefinity focuses on cross-device design, helping to ensure a consistent content experience regardless of user technology.	X	X
Contentstack	Contentstack accelerates and simplifies content management across digital channels, including web, mobile and Internet of Things (IoT).	X	X
Contentful	Contentful is a flexible content platform that helps editors to manage and developers to serve content into mobile or web applications.	X	X

MARKETING AUTOMATION

TOOL/TECHNOLOGY	DESCRIPTION	SMB?	ENTERPRISE?
Act-On	The Act-On Integrated Marketing Platform provides a number of functions, from email marketing to on-site user tracking.	X	X
Salesforce Pardot	B2B marketing automation featuring lead scoring, nurturing, email marketing, and more.		X
HubSpot	HubSpot is an inbound marketing software that focuses on the transformation of marketing from outbound (cold calls, email spam, trade shows, TV ads, and so on) lead generation to inbound lead generation, enabling them to "get found" by more potential customers in the natural course of the way they shop and learn.	X	X
Pega Customer Engagement Suite	Pega helps optimize user engagements with end-to-end automation and real-time artificial intelligence (AI).		X
Marketo	Marketing automation software that helps marketing and sales professionals drive revenue and improve marketing accountability.	X	X
Oracle Eloqua	Oracle Eloqua enables marketers to plan and execute automated marketing campaigns while delivering a personalized customer experience for their prospects.		X
IBM Watson Campaign Automation	IBM Watson Campaign Automation is a digital marketing technology provider that unifies marketing automation, email, mobile, and social.		X
MailChimp	MailChimp helps you design and share campaigns across multiple email and ad channels, integrate with services you already use, and track your results.	X	X

CONTENT ANALYTICS AND INTELLIGENCE

TOOL/TECHNOLOGY	DESCRIPTION	SMB?	ENTERPRISE?
Adobe Analytics	Adobe Analytics helps you create a holistic view of your business by turning customer interactions into actionable insights. With intuitive and interactive dashboards and reports, you can identify problems and opportunities.		X
Google Analytics	Google Analytics not only lets you measure sales and conversions, but also gives you insight into how visitors use your site, how they arrived on your site, and how you can keep them coming back.	X	X
ContentWRX	ContentWRX collects content analytics and customer feedback to offer insight into your content's effectiveness.	X	X
Mention	Create alerts for your brand, your industry, your company, your name, or your competitors and be informed in real time about any mentions on the web and social web.	X	X
Meltwater	Manage and measure a data-driven PR program with hyper-targeted search, pitching, social media, and journalist relations features.		X
Cision	With Cision PR software, reach the right audiences and manage impact of coverage across traditional, digital, and social media.	X	X
ForeSee	ForeSee combines an integrated suite of CX applications to deliver voice of customer insights from your real web users.		X
Qualtrics Research Core	Qualtrics Research Core provides online surveys.		X
Medallia	Medallia's feedback management products are built on technology that's designed to capture users' attention, make solutions clear, and motivate employees to act.		X

CONTENT PLANNING AND CREATION

TOOL/TECHNOLOGY	DESCRIPTION	SMB?	ENTERPRISE?
GatherContent	GatherContent is an online platform designed to help teams easily organize, structure, and produce content.	X	X
NewsCred	NewsCred helps businesses to drive real revenue and engagement by delivering the content their audiences need, want, and share.	X	X
Percolate	Percolate provides a powerful, intuitive software platform to manage all your marketing in one place.		X
Kapost	Kapost manages every step of the content marketing process in a single platform.	X	
Contently	Contently helps companies build loyal audiences by managing the workflow of premium content at scale.	X	X
Hootsuite	With Hootsuite, you can monitor keywords, manage multiple Twitter, Facebook, LinkedIn, Foursquare, Ping.fm, and WordPress profiles, schedule messages, and measure your success.	X	X
Zoho Social	Schedule unlimited posts, manage social networks, track conversations, and measure performance from a single dashboard.	X	X
Falcon.io	Falcon.io enables marketing teams working in HQ, local marketing groups or dealerships, and supporting agencies to collaborate to ensure a consistent brand presence across the different social media types.		X
Curata	Curata provides solutions for curating, planning, and measuring content's impact.	X	X
ScribbleLive	From planning to delivering business results, ScribbleLive is an end-to-end engagement platform.	X	X
Hightail	Share files, collect feedback, and take your creative projects from concept to completion.	X	X
Trello	Trello is a collaboration tool that organizes your projects into cards and boards. In one glance, Trello tells you what's being worked on, who's working on it, and where something is in process.	X	X
Todoist	Todoist for Business helps you and your team stay focused, productive, and in sync by collecting all to-dos, dependencies, and delegations in one place.	X	X

CONTENT OPTIMIZATION

TOOL/TECHNOLOGY	DESCRIPTION	SMB?	ENTERPRISE?
Lucky Orange	Lucky Orange is a tool that lets you quickly see who is onsite and interact with them in many ways		X
Optimizely	The Unbounce feature allows you to build, publish, and A/B test your landing pages without your IT department.	X	X
Instapage	Instapage makes personalized content for teams and agencies by providing an end-to-end solution for quickly building, integrating, and optimizing landing pages.	X	X
VWO	VWO is an A/B testing tool. Tweak, optimize, and personalize your website and apps with minimal IT help.	X	X
Hotjar	All-in-one analytics and feedback.	X	X
Smartlook	Smartlook is a tool that records the screens of real users on your website.	X	X
Crazy Egg	Crazy Egg's heat map and scroll map reports demonstrate how your visitors engage with your website.	X	X
Adobe Experience Manager Contentful ContentWRX MailChimp Pega Customer Engagement Suite	These tools offer a built-in optimization tool or feature set. See their descriptions under previous categories.		

TRAINING

Quality online and in-person training is available for a range of content roles and topics. Additionally, many tools and technologies noted in this appendix offer free or low-cost training about content issues.

ONLINE

- Content Science Academy
- Google Analytics Academy
- Lynda.com (owned by LinkedIn)
- User Interface Engineering's All You Can Learn Library
- The Team W (Susan Weinschenk) online courses

EVENTS

- An Event Apart
- Confab Intensive
- Content Marketing Master Class by Content Marketing Institute
- UI Conferences by User Interface Engineering

READING AND LISTENING

These books, articles, podcasts, and more provide useful insight about a range of content issues. Many of the tools and technologies mentioned earlier in this appendix also offer blogs and free guides that are useful.

ANALYTICS AND CUSTOMER RESEARCH

- *Don't Make Me Think,* by Steve Krug
- *Data Science for Business,* by Foster Provost and Tom Fawcett
- *Predictive Analytics,* by Eric Siegel
- *Jobs to Be Done,* by David Farber, Jessica Wattman, and Stephen Wunker
- *100 Things Every Designer Should Know About People,* by Susan Weinschenk
- Articles under "Content Analysis" and "Content Intelligence" on Content Science Review

CONTENT PLANNING AND CREATION

- *Content Strategy Toolkit,* by Meghan Casey
- *Nicely Said,* by Nicole Fenton and Kate Kiefer Lee
- *Rules,* by Ann Handley
- *Conversation Design,* by Erika Hall
- *Storynomics,* by Robert McGee and Tom Gerace
- *Letting Go of the Words,* by Ginny Redish
- Content Marketing Institute blog

PERSUASION AND INFLUENCE

- *Pre-Suasion,* by Robert Cialdini
- *Influence,* by Robert Cialdini
- *Hooked,* by Nir Eyal
- *How to Get People to Do Stuff,* by Susan Weinschenk

CULTURE (ORGANIZATIONAL)

- *Big Potential,* by Shawn Achor
- *Quiet,* by Susan Cain
- *Leaders Eat Last,* by Simon Sinek
- *Start with Why,* by Simon Sinek

AUTOMATION AND SYSTEMS

- *Algorithms to Live By,* by Brian Christian and Tom Griffiths
- *Thinking in Systems: A Primer,* by Donella Meadows
- *The Fourth Age,* by Byron Reese
- *Intelligent Content,* by Ann Rockley
- *Thinking in Systems,* by Steven Schuster
- Articles under "Automation" on McKinsey Insights
- *Narrative Insights* blog
- The Content Wrangler blog, books, and webinars

STRATEGY AND OPERATIONS

- *Playing to Win: How Strategy Really Works*, by A. G. Lafley and Roger L. Martin
- *Great by Choice*, by Jim Collins and Morten T. Hansen
- *The Founder's Mentality*, by Chris Zook and James Allen
- Articles and reports under "Content Strategy" and "Content Operations" on *Content Science Review*
- Articles under "Strategy" on McKinsey Insights

DECISION MAKING, PERFORMANCE, AND SUCCESS

- *The Happiness Advantage*, by Shawn Achor
- *Before Happiness*, by Shawn Achor
- *Barking Up the Wrong Tree*, by Eric Barker
- *Smarter Faster Better*, by Charles Duhigg
- *Mindset*, by Carol Dweck
- *Grit*, by Angela Duckworth
- *Thinking in Bets*, by Annie Duke
- *Happier* (podcast), hosted by Gretchen Rubin
- *The Four Tendencies*, by Gretchen Rubin
- *The Potential Principle*, by Mark Sanborn

INDEX

• •